REMEMBERING

Lewisboro

REMEMBERING
Lewisboro
NEW YORK

Maureen Koehl

THE History PRESS

Published by The History Press
Charleston, SC 29403
www.historypress.net

First published 2008

Manufactured in the United States

ISBN 978.1.59629.517.9

Library of Congress Cataloging-in-Publication Data

Koehl, Maureen (Maureen L.)
Remembering Lewisboro / Maureen Koehl.
p. cm.
Columns originally published in the Lewisboro ledger since 2000.
ISBN 978-1-59629-517-9
1. Lewisboro (N.Y. : Town)--History--Anecdotes. 2. Lewisboro (N.Y. : Town)--Biography--Anecdotes. I. Title.
F129.L59K64 2008
974.7'277--dc22
2008023773

Notice: The information in this book is true and complete to the best of our knowledge. It is offered without guarantee on the part of the author or The History Press. The author and The History Press disclaim all liability in connection with the use of this book.

Contents

Acknowledgements

Almost eight years of "Window Into History" columns would not have been possible without the support of the readers of the *Lewisboro Ledger*. They read, they questioned and they suggested topics to explore. To the readers, then, and to my family, I dedicate this collection of ramblings into the town of Lewisboro's past.

Introduction

I will let this "Window Into History" column, originally published in December 2004, serve as the introduction to our peek into the history of Lewisboro, New York, a small semirural town in northern Westchester County. I have selected twenty-six columns from among those written over the past eight years that I hope will give the reader a sense of who we are and of those who came before. The first column appeared in the November 22, 2000 issue of the *Lewisboro Ledger*, published by the Hersam-Acorn Newspapers. The last is yet to come.

The history of Lewisboro is the history of its hamlets. There are six in all, stretching from east to west. The ambitious traveler—or today's soccer mom delivering a child to a school chum in the most far-reaching corner of the town—will travel about seventeen miles from Vista to Goldens Bridge, through Lewisboro hamlet, South Salem, Waccabuc and Cross River, or vice versa. Our town includes twenty-eight square miles of rolling hills, rock outcroppings, lakes, fields, babbling streams and housing developments. We can boast of a railroad station, two reservoirs, parts of two county parks, several town parks, serene open spaces, three small shopping centers and cellphone towers (not enough by today's standards). In our 277 years of existence, not much has changed in the overall scheme of things. We are now, and have always been, a collection of individual hamlets—the townsfolk seem to like it that way.

Although Lewisboro is part of New York, much of its eastern half was once considered Connecticut. Even into the early 1970s, folks in the Lewisboro and Vista hamlets enjoyed Connecticut addresses and postal service (Connecticut license plates as well). Many of the founding families in the eastern half of town came inland from the Connecticut coastal towns of Stamford, Norwalk and New Haven. Families migrated to Ridgefield and spilled over into the no man's land of what was to become Lewisboro. We share much of our history with Ridgefield and New Canaan. Eighteenth-

and nineteenth-century family ties were not cut off by state boundaries. The first telephone lines running into South Salem in the last years of the nineteenth century came from Ridgefield. The New Canaan Fire Department fought many a fire in Vista until the Vista Fire Department was established in 1941. There is still a tendency for Vista residents to gravitate toward New Canaan for business and shopping. Many South Salem residents shop, conduct business and attend church in Ridgefield. Even our geography is more akin to that of our New England neighbors. Rocks, rocks and more rocks still define our landscape. As in bygone days, these same boulders provided material for the wonderful stone walls that cross our fields and wander through the woods.

As this eastern area of town was known as part of the Oblong, the western section of town was part of Van Cortlandt Manor. The manor line extended as far east as the western shore of Lake Waccabuc and the eastern edge of the Ward Pound Ridge Reservation, ending near the Tator Garage property. The far western half of town was settled by families coming north from New York City and points in the south, as well as by tenant farmers from the manor land.

Large farms developed in this part of Lewisboro in the 1800s, especially the Brady empire, once the largest dairy farm in Westchester and Putnam Counties. The dairy farms needed easy access to markets. In the 1840s, the railroad arrived to provide that access with freight cars and passenger carriages. Irish workers streamed into our town and those nearby to build the rail lines. Fifty years later, more immigrants (Italian this time) arrived to work on the New York City water-system reservoirs. Blacks also came to the area to drive the mule teams. Still our quiet, almost backwater community carried on as it had for the last hundred years. The western section of Goldens Bridge was sacrificed for the reservoir. A few homes were moved before the flooding and were repositioned along Old Bedford Road. Most of the turn-of-the-century residents welcomed the coming of "the lake," as the old-timers called it. The thought of fishing, picnics and general good times in the hamlet's clean, pure air enticed summer travelers to spend their one-week vacations at one of the several tourist homes and hotels that graced turn-of-the-century Goldens Bridge.

As the railroad effected the first major modern change upon the hamlet of Goldens Bridge, it was followed by the expansion of the north–south highway corridor—first Route 22, then the expanded Route 22 and finally the granddaddy of them all, Interstate 684. The quiet village of Goldens Bridge did not develop into a transportation, shopping and business hub; instead, the ever-increasing bands of cement roadway wiped out what was left of a semidepressed collection of bars, restaurants and shops. Attempts at a full-scale shopping center and a hotel for business travelers never got off the ground or received local support. Instead, housing developments followed the roads north from White Plains and Manhattan. All that remains of the former glory of Goldens Bridge lies hidden across the fast lanes and the Metro-North tracks on Old Bedford Road.

Cross River suffered the same fate as Goldens Bridge with the coming of the twentieth century. Not only were acres of farmland taken for the Cross River Reservoir in 1905, but the center of a thriving country village was also flooded and wiped from memory. This hamlet is indeed a crossroads, where the major road from Bedford and other points south meet Route 35, the main drag running from east to west. Once, several mills, general stores, a blacksmith and two churches graced the hamlet. The churches still stand, but only the Baptist church still holds services each Sunday. What once was pastureland and sumac-covered lowland is now home to hundreds of condominium dwellers in the Meadows. More farmland and a gravel pit have given way to the town's major shopping center and the secondary school complex. The town's first traffic light was installed at the intersection of Routes 35 and 121. As a veteran of the pre–traffic light days, it is hard for me to imagine navigating that intersection with today's traffic flow.

When the land in the area was condemned for the building of a container for New York City's eleven billion gallons of drinking water, most homes and stores were salvaged. A few homes were moved, one all the way to Katonah; the Methodist church was moved to the high ground across the highway to its current resting spot, but most buildings were reduced to lumber that was used elsewhere in the reconstruction of the hamlet. Fifth Division Market is one such building.

The highways are not the only channels to meet in this hamlet—two of the larger rivers in town also cross pathways in Cross River. The Indian River flows past Fifth Division Market into the Cross River, which wends its way westward from Cross Pond (Lake Kitchawan) along the boundary of Pound Ridge Reservation. This river was probably named after John Cross, an early settler in the area. Now the hamlet is the deli and restaurant capital of Lewisboro, having the greatest number of eating places per capita.

Cross River might also have been a railroad crossroads during the heyday of railroad construction in the last quarter of the nineteenth century. At least two railroad companies planned lines through the hamlet. Farmers were eager to sell part of their land to the railroad companies, believing that the convenience of the iron horses would sustain the dairy and farming industries. We should be grateful that most of the would-be railroad companies went belly up before any tracks were laid.

Waccabuc has always been a photogenic and idyllic hamlet, possessing a more leisurely pace off the beaten track. Now known for recreation and relaxation, Mead Street and its environs were home to dairy farms from the late 1700s until the 1950s. First settled by Enoch and Jemima Mead about 1776, Mead Street continued to thrive under the Mead family's influence for almost three centuries. The beautiful Lake Waccabuc is the focal point of the hamlet. It is the deepest lake in the area and is approximately a mile long. Boating, fishing and swimming attracted people escaping the ills of the nineteenth-century city summers. Many of these families became permanent residents of Lewisboro as the years went by. And, no, there is no elephant buried in the depths of the lake!

Lewisboro hamlet has always been the "lost" hamlet, the one hard to identify. It even escaped the Lewisboro mapmakers for a while. The hamlet is the most rural and is still graced by fields, pastures and open land. There are new neighborhoods, built up around new roads, but the feeling one gets driving along Smithridge or Elmwood Roads is one of spaciousness. A hundred years ago, there used to be a post office, a one-room schoolhouse and a church on Kitchawan Road. Time and progress declared them obsolete. The store and school are now private homes and the church is a sculptor's studio. Annie Bell's magnificent home, originally called West Wind, is the home of the Jewish Family Congregation today. The little community that sat along the Mill River, complete with its own tearoom, is a thing of the past. All that one can make out along the banks of the river are the remnants of the millrace and the promise of still more railroad tracks that never made it as far as Lewisboro.

Beautiful St. Paul's Chapel stands watch over the border between Lewisboro hamlet and Vista, lest anyone go astray. Beck Hill Cemetery protects the souls of Lewisboro's and Vista's past citizens.

South Salem, positioned almost at the center of the town, has served as the seat of government for almost three hundred years. Although the present town hall has served only since 1950, the government historically has presided over the residents from somewhere on the hamlet's Main Street. One former post office is now a textile-conservation workshop, while another is a private home. Both of these edifices saw service as town halls at one time. Although serving as the ceremonial center of Lewisboro, the hamlet hasn't been the business hub or shopping attraction that it was in the early nineteenth century. At that time, at least two general stores, a blacksmith, a carriage maker, a wheelwright and a chair maker all vied for the attention of the rural folk. Now, the only rural atmosphere left in downtown South Salem is Echo Farm, with its picturesque horses and the occasional escaped bovine.

More stories exist about this hamlet than about any of the others, thanks to a gentleman named Theodore Van Norden, who first came to South Salem about 1892 as the pastor of the White Church. He soon became involved with real estate. Before he left the town (and the country) for jolly old England, his ideas foreshadowed the beginning of large-scale development in town with the planning and development of Truesdale Lake as a vacation haven. Until 1927, this remarkable gentleman spent years compiling the history of the town. Unfortunately, he wrote mostly about South Salem and did not include the other hamlets. His unpublished manuscript is available at the South Salem Library upon request.

I hope this bird's-eye tour of our town's six hamlets will open your eyes and thoughts to just what makes Lewisboro such a unique place to live. The first 277 years were the easiest. It's our job to keep Lewisboro a fine place to live.

Originally published on March 4, 2004.

Part I

Our Town

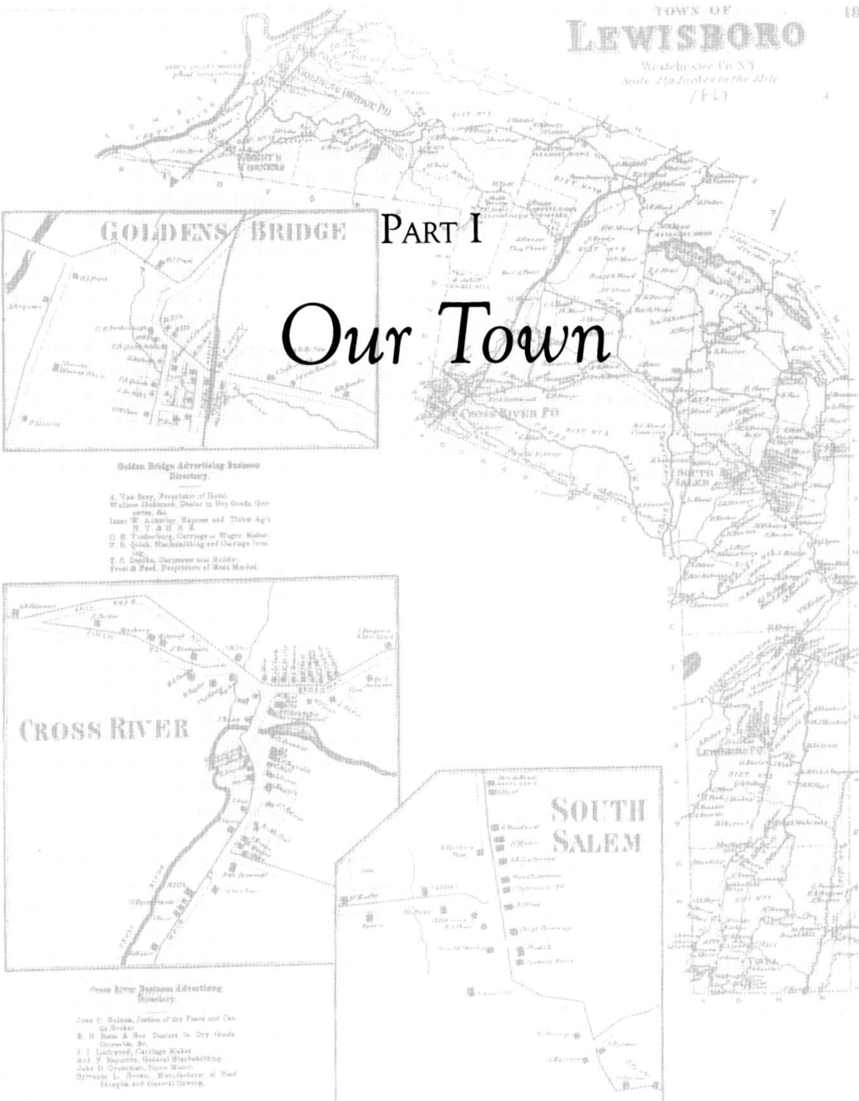

The Oblong

Once upon a time, "heaps of stones" marked the ragged New York–Connecticut border. Relations between New York, Connecticut and Massachusetts are relatively calm nowadays, but it wasn't always so, especially if we journey back to the eighteenth and nineteenth centuries. A unique border dispute raged for more than one hundred years between these three political entities. The settlement of these disputes led to the establishment of the Equivalent Lands, also known as the Oblong.

The story of the Oblong begins with the settlement of the New Haven Colony by the English and the settlement by the Dutch and English of New Netherland and New York, a territory that switched hands and names several times. Confusion arose over the exact dimensions of the territories granted by the different kings since no one actually knew the breadth of the newly colonized continent. The Dutch claimed all lands west of the Connecticut River. The English colony of Connecticut continually pushed its settlements along Long Island Sound until the settled areas reached south of the Byram River to present-day Greenwich.

In September 1654, an agreement reached in Hartford after a loud and angry debate established boundaries between the Dutch and English on Long Island. One line was drawn running from the western part of Oyster Bay to the ocean. Another was drawn running twenty miles inland in a northerly direction from the mainland on the west side of Greenwich Bay. Ten years later, this agreement fell apart when the English conquered New Netherland and established the province of New York. The border debate was then rekindled, this time between the two English settlements. In October 1664, a pact was made to establish the boundaries between New York and Connecticut based on a line running twenty miles east of the Hudson River and running north from Long Island Sound (parallel to the river). The line was to begin at the mouth of the Mamaroneck Creek on the sound and extend in a north-northwesterly direction to the Massachusetts border.

Following this line, surveyors discovered that New York's territory would end below West Point, which was not acceptable to the New Yorkers.

However, with political events in Europe being what they were, the ownership of the New York territory passed back to the Dutch in 1669, but returned again to the English soon after. The border dispute took a political back seat until 1680. In the meantime, Connecticut officials had surveyed the line, beginning with the "new mills erected by Mr. Frederick Philipse" near the present village of Tarrytown and given themselves ample "new" lands. New York officials were not ready to cede all of the territory claimed by this survey crew to their Connecticut neighbors.

Connecticut delegates were sent to parley with New York Governor Dongan in 1683 to settle the boundary dispute once and for all. They requested possession of all the surveyed lands running north-northwest from Mamaroneck. Governor Dongan refused and insisted on keeping the twenty miles from the Hudson line originally agreed upon in 1664. Surveying parameters were set up. The boundary would start at the mouth of the Byram River and run to the head of the tidewater. Then it would run north-northwest for eight miles away from the sound, and finally for another twelve miles parallel to the sound. After that, another line would be drawn running parallel to the Hudson River, twenty miles east of the river, north to the Massachusetts border. A tract of land to the east of this line would be laid aside, equal in area to the land yielded to Connecticut on the shores of Long Island Sound. This parcel came to be known as the Equivalent Lands, or the Oblong. The land to be yielded to Connecticut was calculated to be 61,440 acres. Since the decision was not in Connecticut's favor, few steps were taken to formalize the surveys and the agreement. The border remained as it was—no transfer of territory took place.

In 1717, the government of New York made an effort to enlist Connecticut in the final determination of the border. Since an error of 305 rods occurred in the calculations near the starting point of the "Duke's Tree" ("N" on the Oblong map), giving an unlawful advantage to Connecticut, the surveying process was slowed down until 1725. The eventual settling of this miscalculation led to the familiar Connecticut panhandle, and the town we all know and love as Lewisboro became part of New York and not Connecticut. It also gave Rye and Bedford to New York, and gave the rich oyster beds of Long Island Sound to Connecticut. The settlements of Rye and Bedford were not happy about the switch, preferring the Connecticut form of government to that of the New York colony.

The surveying and mapping began in 1725 and finished in 1731. The boundary was marked by a stone monument erected at the true corner near the Duke's Tree, as determined by the twenty-mile distance from Verplanck's Point on the Hudson River made with random perpendiculars measured at two-mile intervals. These perpendicular lines were marked with little heaps

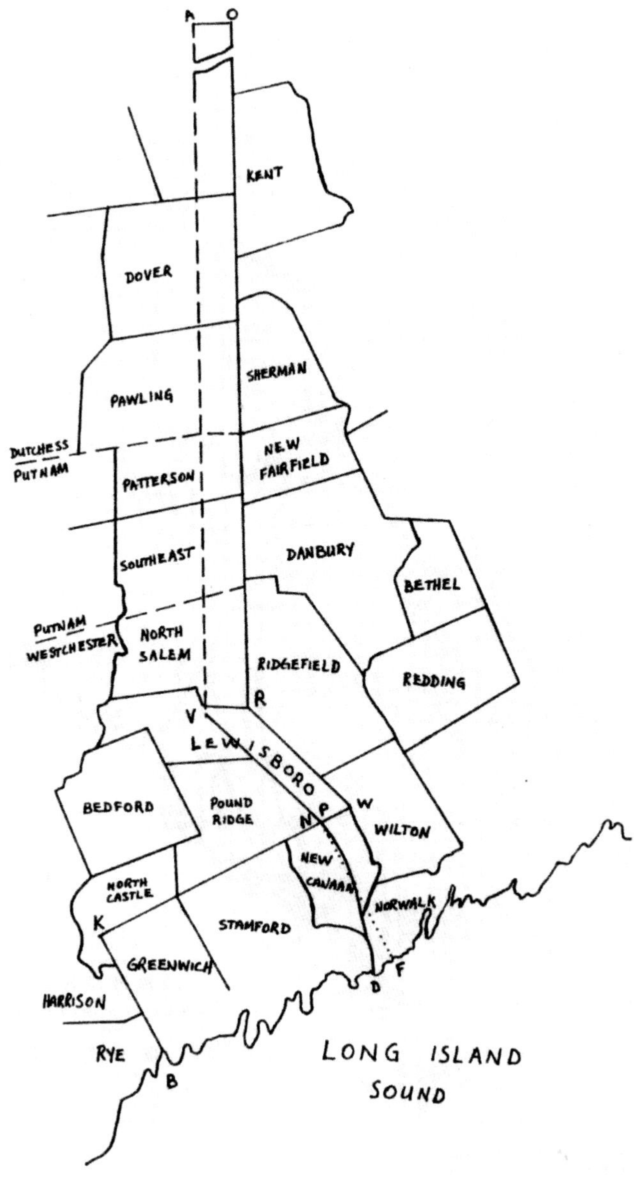

This map of the Oblong appeared in the *New Canaan Historical Society Annual* in June 1951.

of stones. The area of the Equivalent Lands, measured in this fashion to the Massachusetts border, was determined to be one and three-quarter miles wide (plus an additional twenty rods) and about fifty miles long. Little heaps of stone marked this oblong area along its entirety. These piles of stones were placed on vacant land, pastureland and steep mountainsides.

The boundary was anything but straight, maybe because the survey party carried an ample supply of rum and lime juice along with their quadrants, hooks and lines. An excerpt from the *New Canaan Historical Society Annual* (Vol. III, June 1951) states that supplies included "16 and one-half gallons of Rum, 13 lbs. loaf sugar, 1 lb. cinnamon, 1 oz. nutmeg, one and one-half gallons lime juice, six and one-half gallons brandy, 350 limes, eight shillings worth of tobacco and pipes, and two shillings worth of hooks and lines." Is it any wonder that mistakes were made given those ingredients, which were worthy of cocktail parties as the sun went down each evening.

About 1850, the errors in the 1731 measurement were discovered by Connecticut officials and controversy broke out again. In 1860, the New York State legislature empowered the New York boundary commissioners to resurvey the boundary line established in 1731 and mark it with permanent marble markers. They gave their Connecticut counterparts one month's notice to join the survey party, but there was no response from the Connecticut commissioners, so the New Yorkers went alone. They placed eight-inch-square, two-foot-high marble markers at prominent places and road crossings along the border. Some of these markers can still be found, notably on the Bulkley estate, on a spot not far from Sarah Bishop's cave and on Pumping Station Road. This 1860 survey *almost* provided the final decision when it was ratified by both state legislatures in 1880 and 1881. As late as 1980, Governors Ella Grasso and Hugh Carey discussed petitions raised by Dutchess County residents in Millerton to change their local section of the border.

If the reader meandered through all the verbiage up to this point, perhaps some local landmarks would help explain just what the Oblong means to Lewisboro. For the most part, it means that we are New Yorkers, although much of our heritage belongs to Connecticut. The Equivalent Lands stretched to the southwestern shore of Lake Waccabuc and to the eastern boundary of Van Cortlandt Manor. All of Vista, Lewisboro hamlet and South Salem were part of the Oblong. Most of the rest of the town was included in Van Cortlandt lands until 1788.

For all practical purposes, the eastern and southern boundaries were set in 1731, before the town of Salem was established. Many of the original landholders and settlers of Salem bought land from the Reverend Thomas Hawley of Ridgefield, who was the leading land speculator of the day and who worked a deal to lay claim to more than fifty thousand acres of the Oblong.

Originally published on February 21, 2003.

Salem Bans Smallpox Inoculations and the "Nefarious" Dr. Abbott

For the first 150 years or more, our town subscribed to the New England Town Meeting style of government, holding its annual town meeting early in April. Only on special occasions were additional meetings called for during the course of the year. Reading through the leather-bound record books of our town's early history, one can travel quickly through the years. Every now and then, special meetings were held to deal with a specific problem facing the populace. Smallpox inoculation was the subject of a special meeting called in January 1763. In the eighteenth century, smallpox caused much alarm to our forefathers and foremothers and was a subject of concern throughout New England in the 1700s. Isn't it curious that three hundred years later, that most horrible of diseases is once again in our thoughts? John Adams described smallpox as "ten times more terrible than Britons, Canadians and Indians together." And English poet Thomas Macaulay called it "the most terrible of all the ministers of death." It was rightly feared by everyone.

The following excerpts were taken from the town records of Salem. An explanation follows, but first, through the words recorded by Salem's town "clark," Abijah Gilbert, we find ourselves transported to the winter of 1763. The reader can sense the concern the inhabitants of Salem have for the idea of "inoccilation," which has recently crossed the border and now threatens the town.

> *January 10, 1763*
>
> *At Town Meeting Legally Warned & met at the School house in Salem this 10 Day of Jany. 1763. To Consider of such matters & pass Such Votes as may be for the Wellfare of the Town. This Meeting being Informed that one Doctor Michael Abbott of Ridgfield in the Colony of Connecticut hath Lately Come into this place with sundry other persons from the Colony of Connecticut...The aforesaid Abbott hath Enokilated with the Small pox at the house of one Gershom Sillick which house Stands on a publick Highway in this place by means whereof the people are Greatly Exposed & put in much Danger of Taking the Small Pox.*

This meeting taking the matter of the aforesaid Information in to their Consideration and apprehending Great Damag of having the Small pox Spread by means of Such unjust proceedings and that under the present Circumstances of this place Such a Distemper being Spred among us would be attended with most fatal consequences by Reason of the Great number of poor people among us that are not by any means able to pay the Charges for inoccilation of themselves & families and must Inevitable Suffer in Case it Should Spread among them and in Consideration of our having at all times when the Small pox happened among us Used our Greatest Care and Caution to prevent the Spreading thereof by Removing people who have taken it into our houses So that it is Supposed that not one to thirty of the Inhabitants Ever had it. This meeting thinks it is Contrary to natural Right as Well as the Intentions of the Law which is Calculated for the peace and Safety of all his majesties Subjects that they Should be thus Exposed and Endangered in their Lives and Estates to Gratifie the avaricious Inclinations of a Doctor or Doctors from the Colony of Connecticut.

For the Reasons above this meeting Unanimously Vote that no person or persons from the Colony of Connecticut be Suffered to Communicate or Receive the Small pox by way of Inoccilation within this town…Such as have allready presumed to Introduce the Small pox in that way Contrary to the forbiddance of the Justice or Justices of this place or that Shall hereafter Introduce it be prosecuted for the Same & that this meeting by their Vote now passed Do make themselves Complainants against those who have allready Received it as well as against the Doctor who Communicated it & Do further appoint a Committee of Samll Brown Benjamin Close & Nathan Osborn to appear and prosecute the afore Said Complaint in behalf of this meeting.

The devastating smallpox virus had been known since the time of the Egyptian pharaohs, circa 3700 BC, and had probably traveled to Europe from Africa along the trade routes. The disease most likely reached America's shores with the Spaniards. Early in the 1700s, Europeans learned that naturally occurring smallpox could be prevented by inducing a deliberate infection via the skin. Doctors in England secretly experimented with techniques of transferring the disease from infected persons to healthy ones. However, skepticism outweighed belief in the control of the disease.

In New England, in the early 1720s, two men stood out as proponents of inoculation as a prevention of the spread of the disease. Famed Puritan minister Cotton Mather was a firm believer in the practice, having learned about it from his African slave, Onesimus. A physician in the Boston area,

A 1930 aerial view of Onatru Farm shows the Alice Poor home. Originally the Gershom Silleck home, the eighteenth-century farmhouse is the focal point of a town park.

Dr. Zabdiel Boylston, carried on Reverend Mather's crusade, experimenting with his own son, Thomas. Of the 240 people he inoculated, 6 died. The rest survived, suffering either no symptoms at all, or just a mild case of them. Dr. Boylston inoculated a patient by scratching the skin of a healthy person with a sharp instrument that had been dipped into the pock (pustule) of an infected person. The resulting infection usually caused a minor case of smallpox in the healthy person but protected him from contracting the disease again.

Although the idea of inoculation traveled throughout the colonies, the practice was greatly feared and, as we can see in the case of Salem, not welcomed in many communities for fear the disease would be spread, not contained, and that inoculation would harm more than it would help. Obviously, by 1763, the controversy had reached as far as our little backwater village and Dr. Abbott of Ridgefield Town was not welcomed with open arms.

While physicians were trying to prevent the dreaded malady, the British army was using the virus as one of its deadliest weapons. The British were masters of biological warfare in their skirmishes with the Native Americans in the French and Indian Wars between 1754 and 1763. Lord Jeffrey Amherst (namesake of Amherst, Massachusetts, and the college of the same name) was the biggest proponent. He devised the devilish scheme of sending infected blankets into the Native American camps. The natives had no immunity to the disease and the British had developed stronger resistances, having lived with smallpox for centuries. Most tribes were devastated by the disease as the quickly spreading, rapidly debilitating sickness took hold in villages. Infection was transferred by inhaling the virus from the exhalations of an infected person, from his clothing or from his bedding.

In his May 24, 1763 journal entry, William Trent, commander of the local militia at Fort Pitt during an Indian encounter known as Pontiac's Rebellion, proudly admits, "We gave them two Blankets and an Handkerchief out of the Small Pox Hospital. I hope it will have the desired effect."

It was not until Dr. Edward Jenner noticed the "milkmaid phenomenon" at the close of the century that the scourge of smallpox was finally on its way to being eradicated. He developed his "cowpox" vaccine in 1796, thirty-three years after the Salem town meeting.

Originally published on December 6, 2001.

The Eponymous John Lewis

John Lewis was born on February 4, 1793, in Salem (as our town was known until 1806). He was the third son of John Lewis of Clinton, Connecticut, and Peggy Hayes Lewis of Salem. Peggy Hayes was the daughter of Isaac Hayes, a prominent Salem farmer. The Hayes farm was near the southern end of Elmwood Road. The house John Lewis was born in on that cold February day is no longer standing. We don't know if John Lewis actually lived in his grandfather's house during his early childhood or if he grew up in Clinton. Sources say that his father "removed to South Salem" from Clinton in 1808. John would have been fifteen then. Maybe the family traveled back and forth between the two towns and came to Salem to live permanently when Peggy's father died in 1805. However, it is Peggy, not her husband, who is listed as the head of household in the 1810 census. She is not listed in the 1820 census because she died in 1819.

Wherever John Lewis spent his youth, he moved to Darien sometime before 1814 to work as a clerk for Captain Isaac Jones. Captain Jones was a merchant and the owner of the schooner *Clio* that "carried goods, wares and merchandise and the produce of the country to New York." A one-way trip took anywhere from twelve to twenty-four hours in 1810. Captain Jones died in 1814, and according to Bolton's *History of the County of Westchester*, John Lewis "removed to Danbury and not long after that to New York City."

In New York City, Lewis went to work for Hoffman and Sons, a well-known auctioneering house. After three years of dedicated service, John Lewis opened his own business on Wall Street, "where, by his untiring energy and perseverance, he amassed a large fortune," according to *History of the County of Westchester*. He was listed as a "broker" in the New York City business directory for the years 1833–49. In 1851, John Lewis invested in a large amount of property in Clinton, Connecticut. The area is now in the town of Westbrook on the shore of Long Island Sound. At that time, in local newspapers, he was referred to as a retired New York City banker.

John Lewis married Mary Bishop of Darien. She was the daughter of prominent Hicksite Quakers and active in Quaker activities in the Darien-Stamford area. I have found no date for the couple's marriage and they had no children. Mary died in 1852, shortly after John's retirement. About this time, Lewis wrote a book, *The Merits of Protestantism Demonstrated by the Character of Man and His History in Various Countries from the Earliest Recorded Period to the*

Present Century. He may have been living in Clinton at this time. He was living in Washington, D.C., at the time of his death on October 1, 1871.

Even in death, John Lewis presents a mystery. He is buried next to his mother in a plot in the Beck Hill Cemetery. His wife is buried with her parents in Darien. I have not been able to locate the grave of John Lewis's father. Nothing is known about John Lewis Sr. except that he served in the Revolutionary War.

Since John and Mary Lewis had no children, John's nephew, William Isaac Lewis, of Clinton, inherited the estate, including the Lewis farm on the Connecticut shore that John had bought twenty years earlier. William Lewis was an official in the post office department in Washington, D.C. It is possible that John Lewis was living with his nephew at the time of his death.

There are many more questions concerning our mysterious Mr. Lewis. Why was he buried with his mother and not with his wife? Where is his father? Why did he offer $10,000 to his "hometown" if he hardly ever lived here? The final curiosity is contained in his last will and testament.

John Lewis's will contained another veiled clue to his life and personality, declaring:

> *Having witnessed the great evil of intemperance, and having suffered pecuniarily and in feeling and mortification from intemperance from others, I especially direct and require that no part of my estate should be expended for the support of drunkenness, directly or indirectly!*

To add an ironic twist to this story, William Lewis shared his uncle's business sense and developed the farm he inherited from his uncle into a summer resort in the 1880s. In 1906, he added Duck Island to his holdings. The entire area then become known (and still is known) as Grove Beach. William Lewis had sold the Duck Island property by the 1920s. It is interesting to note, in light of the proviso in John Lewis's will, that Duck Island became a popular landing spot for bootlegging smugglers during Prohibition. An endless, clandestine fleet of small boats docked on the island every night. Perhaps some of the grandest secret parties in U.S. history can be traced to the "liquid gold" brought ashore on former Lewis property.

It's amazing how the Internet has managed to bring people closer to their genealogical roots. If it works for people, it can work for towns as well. Tipped off by a South Salem resident to the wonders of searching for out-of-print books via the Internet, I decided to try a search on John Lewis and the book he wrote in 1852. Lo and behold! To the wonder of my little blue eyes, there appeared before me on the computer screen the very book I was seeking—a first degree of separation to the name-giver of our town.

We had no other tangible evidence of this man's existence. Now we have one small link to John Lewis in the form of a little brown book—five by seven inches in size and 491 pages of very small print and very brown edges. *Merits, etc.* was published by C. Welford of No. 7 Astor House in New York in 1852. The only trouble seems to be that this book is the fourth of five volumes. Mr. Lewis was preparing a fourth edition of this popular tome at the time of his death. The book contains seventy-six chapters, beginning with the history of the Athenians, extending up to the history of the Taxiles—pretty heady stuff. While not exactly light reading, the book defends Protestantism against the advances of popery and the dangers of Roman Catholicism, as proved through myriad histories of civilizations that are detailed in the book.

Needless to say, John Lewis was a man with strong religious principles. He was a great benefactor of the Episcopalian Church and donated the money to build St. Paul's Chapel in Vista, near his grandfather's homestead. He also stipulated that the chapel be named St. Paul's.

For the most part, John Lewis, namesake of our town—the man who pledged $10,000 in 1840 for South Salem public schools if the town would change its name to Lewisboro—remains an enigma. Who he approached and how the name change was approved seems unrecorded. In April of

After John Lewis's $10,000 gift to the town, the name was changed to Lewisboro; the funds also provided for schoolchildren, seen here in this 1921 South Salem school picture.

1839, at the annual town meeting, the town was referred to as South Salem; the minutes of the April 1840 town meeting refer to Lewisboro, "lately South Salem." It was as simple as that.

A bill was passed in Albany on February 13, 1840, stating:

> *The town of South Salem, in the county of Westchester, shall hereafter be called and known by the name of Lewisboro. Nothing contained in this act shall in any way affect the rights of any inhabitant or officer of said town, or of any other person, or of the town itself. This act shall take effect immediately.*

Originally published on April 18, 2002.

NIMBY, United Nations

Peace is a wonderful thing, but not if it means losing one's home, farm or livelihood, or if it means the wholesale annihilation of towns and villages in the Westchester-Fairfield area.

Most of us are familiar with the tall, slim United Nations building that commands a position on the East River in Manhattan. We grew up with it and visited it as schoolchildren. But did you know that Lewisboro had a very slight chance of becoming the home of the United Nations Organization (as it was known early in its career)? Our sleepy little postwar community was on the shortlist of fifteen sites proposed by the site-selection committee of the UNO in 1946. The area, known as 40-C, was thus described:

> *Starting at the intersection of Route 123 at the New York-Connecticut state line, thence southwest along the line to the east bank of the Mianus Gorge; thence north along the east bank of the Mianus Gorge to the intersection of Ridge Road and River Road; thence northerly along Ridge Road to its intersection with Poundridge Road; thence northerly west of Indian Hill along Kingdom Road to its intersection with Route 121; thence north along 121 to its intersection with Route 35; thence east along Route 35 to its intersection with Route 33; thence southerly along Route 33 to Hendersons Road; thence southwest to the corner intersection of the New York-Connecticut state line to the starting point.*

This area encompassed 7,210 acres in Lewisboro and included the entire hamlets of Vista and Lewisboro as well as land in South Salem and Cross River—991 taxable parcels, 360 residences and 687 building lots. The assessed valuation of the affected territory in site 40-C was: $1,747,000 for land and $1,446,750 for improved properties, for a grand total assessment valuation of $3,193,750. The 1940 census listed 302 families, with 900 to 1,000 people expected to be displaced if the land was condemned or somehow taken by the United Nations. The landmass represented ten square miles, one-third of the area of Lewisboro. The town's population at that time was between 2,500 and 3,000 people. Many families earned their income from agriculture, or were tradesmen, artisans or laborers. Some residents commuted to New York City and other nearby cities like Stamford or White Plains, as they still do today.

A site-selection committee was set up not long after the San Francisco meeting that launched the United Nations Organization in 1945. By February 1946, the wheels had been set in motion to select a site anywhere from two square miles to forty square miles in area for an international conclave. The idea was to have a central governmental zone for the "governmental buildings" in which to house the UN Assembly, Security Council and the secretariat. The remaining area would be a buffer zone so that no towns or cities could encroach on UN territory. Homes for the foreign diplomats would be purchased or built for all of the organization's members in this buffer zone that would probably include stores, schools, theaters, hotels and other amenities as well. Officials estimated that close to five thousand people would inhabit the buffer zone.

The site-selection committee was headed by Dr. Stoyan Gavrilovic of Yugoslavia. By July 1946, the committee had pinpointed fifteen sites: seven in Westchester, three in Fairfield County and five that traversed the two counties' borders. There were three sites in each of the following categories: forty square miles, twenty square miles, ten square miles, five square miles and two square miles. One site in each of the categories was finally chosen. (For comparison, Manhattan is about twenty square miles in size.) Meanwhile, great debates were happening back in the London headquarters of the organization regarding the possibility of locating the permanent headquarters in San Francisco, Philadelphia or Boston. Russia refused to consider the West Coast and other nations were not in favor of the East Coast. Not an auspicious beginning, to be sure. However, Dr. Gavrilovic trudged on, exploring northern Westchester County and Fairfield County, quite aware of the local citizens' resentment at the possibility of being forced off their land and out of their family homes, not to mention the resentment of the loss of area country clubs, the Westchester County Airport, the Westchester Airport (in Armonk, for you old-timers) and the estates of many of the wealthiest landowners in the area.

The long list of selected sites included the following Westchester towns: Harrison, North Castle, Bedford, Rye, Lewisboro, Pound Ridge, Somers, Cortlandt and New Castle. Ridgefield, Wilton, Stamford and Greenwich in Connecticut were also to be affected.

Westchester County Executive Herbert C. Gerlach favored a plan to locate the UN headquarters in Westchester County. He perceived the project as the biggest thing to ever have happened in Westchester and saw it in a positive light, despite the loss of tax revenue (the UN would be exempt from taxes). Some Fairfield County officials felt the same way. The town of Stamford actively pursued the organization, to the distress of its Greenwich and Westchester neighbors. Although Mr. Gerlach welcomed the potential newcomers to the neighborhood, many of the members of the board of supervisors did not. In those days, each town supervisor sat on the county legislative body, unlike nowadays, when Westchester is governed by the board of legislators.

Lewisboro Town Supervisor Hugh S. Coyle firmly opposed the idea and sent the following telegram (a 1940s-style e-mail, for the younger crowd!) to UN Secretary General Trygue Lie:

> *On behalf of the Town of Lewisboro Westchester County New York and with approval of its Town Board I protest selection of area for UNO world capital known as North Stamford Site and the method of selection thereof. I oppose location or possible location in Town of Lewisboro or any part or in any portion of Westchester County. Feb. 3, 1946.*

A citizens committee opposed to the coming of the UN was formed in April 1946 and a poll was taken. Results showed that 383 families were opposed; 51 were in favor of deeding over their land to the new peace organization.

In August 1946, the town sent a questionnaire to all property owners and residents in the affected area. The questions came from UN Headquarters Commission and included the following:

1. *What would be your reaction if U.N. were established in the area in which you are residing? (Favorable, not favorable)*
2. *Number of persons living in your home?*
3. *Place of employment?*

4. *In case the final decision would locate the U.N. in the area in which you are living: Will you oppose the taking of your property? Will you voluntarily sell your property for whatever you can get?*
5. *Will your family consider living within the boundaries of the U.N. if the U.N. would give you the permission to stay for some time?*

Approximately 200 questionnaires were returned from the 300 families living in the area targeted. The results listed 28 neutral, 26 favorable and 146 opposed. I will share some of the comments written on the bottom of the returned questionnaires. Several of the remarks are especially poignant, considering the sentiments and the ensuing fifty-six years.

Thomas Lander of East Street said, "In no manner or method, would I consider opposing the mere hope of a world peace, no matter what my personal opinion might be."

Colonel Alexander Piper of Route 124 said he was in favor "if subject to at least one year's notice to vacate."

Charles Richmond of Lake Kitchawan suggested that the UN buy the properties and give the owner a ninety-nine-year lease with one-dollar-per-year renewal privileges.

The Ruscoe home still survives, much changed, on East Street in Vista. It would have been included in the UN property takeover.

The "no's" predominated, however, and here are a few of them. "No. I have built my home with the idea of living here the rest of my life," World War II veteran Leo Gustavson said adamantly. (Mr. Gustavson did just that, dying several years ago at his Cross River home.)

George Tator of South Salem said, "My family will live according to my suggestions and not by the U.N. We are satisfied to live as Americans should live and do not believe Europe should be permitted to dictate to us. Voluntarily sell? Absolutely not!"

"We expect to live here the rest of our lives," said Jared Pidgeon of East Street. (The Pidgeons did live in Vista for many more years, and then moved to California, where Mr. Pidgeon died in his nineties, a wonderful old gentleman.)

Mrs. Thomas Smith of East Street stated, "I would be disgusted if the U.N. came here."

Stanley Reynolds of Lewisboro answered question number five as many did: "Yes, I would be willing to stay in my home if given permission by the U.N. because there would be no other place to go."

R. Curt and Mildred Hasenclever of Lewisboro said, "What other choice would we have, but to stay? Where, in these times, would it be possible to find a home?"

Mrs. Martha R. Coleman of West Street offered another solution: "It seems to me that the Pound Ridge Reservation and other unoccupied land in the neighborhood should be sufficient without taking our homes."

To bring a very long story to a swift conclusion, all we needed was a Rockefeller! By December 1946, the site-selection committee was still undecided. President Truman, it was rumored, favored Philadelphia. Nelson A. Rockefeller had been appointed by New York City Mayor William O'Dwyer to the committee to convince it to select a Manhattan site. When Nelson got wind of Truman's preference, he called his father, John D. Jr., who offered the UNO either the Rockefeller estate at Pocantico Hills plus one thousand additional contiguous acres, or $8.5 million to buy a nice piece of real estate that had just come on the market bordering the East River. William Zeckendorf had acquired the option to buy the property to build a "dream city," including an airport terminal, hotel, opera house and apartment complex. With a little Rockefeller money, it could be theirs. Another committee was formed to investigate the offer and the site. Within a week, the question of the site for the UN permanent headquarters was settled and we all know the rest of the story!

Originally published on May 2, 2002.

Dining Out Along Roadside Lewisboro

Our town has a long gastronomic history. This quick peek at a few of our well-known local establishments is meant to offer a glimpse into a small part of Lewisboro's gustative past. Nowadays, Le Chateau is the eatery with more than just a local reputation for elegance and quality. Patrons travel for miles from lower Westchester and nearby Connecticut to dine in the turn-of-the-century mansion built for the minister of financier J.P. Morgan. On the southeast side of town, down Vista way, L'Europe entices travelers with its reputation for delicious victuals. While Le Chateau has maintained an elegant distance throughout its history, probably because it has a commanding hillside presence and stays just out of reach of the thousands of passersby along Route 35, L'Europe has worked its way up from a working-class neighborhood gathering place and watering hole to today's reincarnation as a fine French restaurant.

Located in Vista, on Smith Ridge Road, this attractive eatery has a long history of serving the public. Before it became L'Europe, the restaurant was known as the Hearth, and before that, this roadside stop was called the Anvil. The restaurant was geographically well placed. In a no man's land between South Salem and New Canaan, the popular bar was often a rendezvous for Connecticut teenagers when that state and New York had slightly different legal drinking ages. Located in the boonies, there was no local constabulary to patrol the lonesome stretch of highway and the state police were few and far between. Eighteen-year-olds in New York had the drinking privileges the Connecticut youngsters envied, and many were the nights that Lewisboro Justice of the Peace Alvin Jordan was called out of bed to arraign an unruly youth or two. Not all the noisy ones were out-of-towners, however, and local residents praised the day that the State of New York raised the drinking age to twenty-one.

The Hearth (and before that, the Anvil) was a favorite stopping-off place for sandwiches and an after-work beverage or two of choice. The eatery wasn't always the scene of rowdy after-hours behavior. It was also a neighborhood gathering spot.

During Prohibition, it was probably possible to drink one's way from New Canaan to Cross River, and those were the days before designated drivers, so thank heavens the roads were traveled less then and cars were slower—less chance of a serious accident. An adventuresome bootleg buyer could

Koch's Log Cabin in Cross River did a thriving business with the hunting crowd and locals who kept their own cups hanging on the wall.

KOCH'S LOG CABIN
GERMAN COOKING – DANCING
REFRESHMENTS
ICE CREAM

begin his libations in Vista, continue by making a few stops at establishments along Smithridge Road and at small grocery stores (where the booze was kept under the counter or in the backroom) and then continue to Spring Street to an establishment purportedly owned by the notorious Dutch Schultz. About a mile farther, Sfondrini's South Salem Hotel beckoned, where three knocks on the door could get you "one more for the road." Just east of the hotel, Mae Brock hung a sign out on her log cabin roadhouse that read "Ice Cream." If the tales have any truth to them, she served more than ice cream! Spring Street was a happening place. Mae's home and the hotel are now private homes. The log cabin burned down in a spectacular, suspicious fire one windy evening about thirty years ago, so little is left of that colorful history.

The Sfondrini family later moved the Bacon family's barn from its Spring Street home to Route 35 and opened what would be South Salem's most popular restaurant during the forties, fifties, sixties and early seventies. Known as the Hayloft, it provided many a townie and traveler with a pleasant bite to eat.

Cross River has also sported its share of taverns and restaurants from Colonial times right up to the present. Probably one of the most popular establishments was Koch's Log Cabin, which sat on the corner now occupied by the Shell gas station. Many old-time Cross River residents have fond memories of the log cabin, which was a gathering place for locals as well as the steady stream of hunters who came through the area each fall. Several people have mentioned that regulars kept their own coffee mugs on the log cabin's shelf. Area natives like Carl Madsen and Alton Moore remember the establishment well from their boyhood. Both men praised the cooking of Mrs. Koch, especially her baked goods. The day-old goods were just as tasty, at least to a hungry teenager.

Alton Moore of Cross River described the log cabin to me a while back. There was a bar in front and restaurant seating in the back. Ice cream and soda were favorites of the younger set. Mr. Moore said that he and his Boy Scout buddies used to meet at Koch's for a Coke and then walk to Lewisboro Elementary School for their meetings. The Reynolds sisters remember being treated to ice cream cones on their birthdays or on other special occasions, but the log cabin seemed to be more of a boy's hangout than a girl's.

Mr. Moore also speculated that the logs for the cabin may have come from Pound Ridge Reservation and Bill Whitman's sawmill. He said his father and grandfather helped to build the restaurant, probably in the 1920s. Karl and Charlotte Koch bought the log cabin from millionaire sportsman Frank Terhune in September 1931, according to a note in an undated newspaper clipping. They operated the popular restaurant for several decades and then sold the business to a Mr. Campbell. At one point, there was a cider mill behind the log cabin that processed the apples that grew in orchards on the Four Winds property and where John Jay High School now stands.

Koch's Log Cabin commanded the intersection where Routes 121 and 35 meet. Its reputation for hospitality and good food was known far and wide. It was of an era when life was slower. Log cabins were in style until the 1960s. Now all of them are gone. Burger King and McDonald's just don't have the same ambience.

Originally published on December 12, 2004.
(Note: Still under the same ownership, L'Europe is now the Tosca Café in 2008.)

Part II

Vista and Lewisboro

Alice Beers Bauer's Tales of Old Vista

In 1969, Alice Beers Bauer, mother of Hans Bauer of West Road, Vista, wrote down in a scrapbook a wonderful history of the Vista she knew spending summers there as a girl. She included the tales told by her grandfather, Ambrose Abbott Beers, to his son (Alice's father), Lester Irving Beers. The memories Alice prepared for her own grandchildren offer the rest of us a wonderful window into the comings and goings of the Vista of a century ago. We will share a few of these vignettes.

The Beers homestead sits on the east side of West Road, just south of Hack Green Road. When the house was built in the early 1840s, the road ended at Hack Green Road, but with the help of a team of horses and a few neighbors, Jonathan Beers, the highway master at the time, broke through a road to Puddin' Hill. The road was called Jacklin Road, named for a slave owned by Samuel Comstock. Jacklin and his wife lived in a cabin on the Comstock property, near the intersection of the new road and Puddin' Hill. The pair was freed after the Civil War and both are said to be buried by their cabin near the northeast corner of the intersection. The huge Comstock property was contiguous to the Beers land. Being the neighborly sort, old Sam Comstock often loaned out his oxen team, but we'll let Alice tell the story in her own words.

> *Every year Ambrose B. hired a team of oxen from Sam Comstock to plow up the back lot for a garden. When your great-grandfather, Lester, was about ten years old, he begged his father to let him drive the oxen home alone. They were hitched to a two-wheeled cart and were driven by walking along by their head and yelling "gee" (right) and "haw" (left) and by snapping a whip above their backs.*
>
> *The boy and the oxen started sedately down the road—oxen normally move slowly. Then Lester suddenly decided that it would be more fun if he could get them going faster—so he cracked the whip and let out a yell. The oxen started running full sped and tore down the road getting completely away from him.*

Alice Beers Bauer as an infant, resting in the arms of her father, Lester, while her mother looks on. Photo was taken circa 1900.

Greatly frightened, Lester ran "across lots" to head them off on Puddin' Hill as they ran for home. Going up the little hill to the main road, they slowed down to a walk and 10-year old great grandpa caught up to them.

He didn't try to hurry them anymore.

Shoemaking was a local industry from the time of the Revolutionary War or earlier. Most shoes were made as piecework during the winter, the farmer's "time off" from farming chores. He and his family would sit by the fireplace, where it was warm, and sew the cut-out pieces of leather. Then a shoemaker, perhaps Eli Keeler in South Salem, would gather the pieces, add the soles and cart the finished product off to New York City. (Ambrose Beers was also involved in the shoemaking trade.)

By the mid- to late nineteenth century, Vista had its very own shoe factory. It was located in the Vista Market building, which was the general store back then, too. The upper floor housed the shoe factory. Once again, we'll let Alice tell about it in her own words.

> *The factory, store and post office were run by E.L. Fancher and his son A. Fancher. The father ran the factory upstairs and the son ran the store, the post office and finished the shoes (lined, put on eyelets and boxed them).*
>
> *Huge sheets of leather hung in the cutting room (first floor) where soles were cut out by sharp dies of different sizes, struck by a heavy mallet. Only women's shoes were made.*
>
> *There were two rooms on the second floor of the building. In the back room (east end) women sewed all sections of uppers together on machines. In the front room, men put on soles and heels.*
>
> *The front porch of the store was a loading platform, high enough for wagons to back up to and load or unload. The store was later moved back a bit and lowered.*

Molasses and little boys naturally went together in the old days. Anything sweet was worth the effort that went into procuring it. We'll let Alice tell about a favorite after-school treat. Remember that the school was not more than a stone's throw from the general store.

> *Empty (?) molasses barrels were rolled out into the yard in back of the store. Your great grandfather, Lester Beers, and his friends, when school was dismissed, would quickly cut a long stick from a nearby tree or bush and race down to the store yard. There they would feast on the brown sugar and molasses which had settled to the bottom of the barrels. Each boy, in turn, shoved his stick through the bung-hole of the upended barrel, gave it a couple of twists and brought it up dripping ambrosia. There was sometimes as much as a foot of sugary molasses left in the barrel.*

One of the hidden treasures of the Vista hamlet is Mud Pond (also Tommy's Pond or, if you prefer its official name, Lake Siscowit). Old-timers knew it as one of the best places to fish during a summer evening and Alice and her family often visited the pond. The body of water joins the towns of Lewisboro and New Canaan and is part of the Stamford water supply. In Alice's time, it was a wonderful place to spend a warm evening and she describes the splendor and peacefulness of the area:

> *The beauty and tranquility of Mud Pond is one of the treasured memories of my childhood. Dad, Mother and I often fished, toward evening, from the old wooden bridge on the east side, watching the changing beauty of the sky at sunset, the silent flight of the wild ducks and helldivers close above the water, the splashing of fish jumping for water bugs and hearing the crescendos of night sounds, frogs croaking and splashing, insects buzzing and night birds calling.*

What a beautiful picture she paints of a summer's evening on one of our lakes.

Originally published on January 26, 2006.

Elmwood Avenue, Circa 1910

An undated article from an unknown newspaper provided the impetus for this look into Lewisboro history. The article was probably written in the early 1900s. Entitled "Interesting Description of the Houses Along Elmwood Avenue," the writer describes his journey northward on what we now call Elmwood Road, along the entire two-mile course of the roadway beginning near St. Paul's Chapel and ending near the gray saltbox at the intersection with West Lane.

According to the article, the road was named by Charles A. Raymond because of all the elm trees that grew on either side of the roadway. St. Paul's graceful late Victorian chapel, "consecrated on June 12, 1900," sits at the road's intersection with the state highway that runs to New Canaan. A short way down Elmwood Avenue on the right-hand side stands the "upright rock nine feet high, that tradition bequeaths to us as the point reached by the Indians in claiming their lands as far as they could walk in a day starting from Stamford."

This boulder at the south end of Elmwood Road is said to mark the distance from the coast an American Indian could walk in a day.

Just beyond the rock, also on the right, is Laffalot, the home of William Henry Bouton; the home of Miss Lucy Raymond sits on the other side of the street. The tale is told that Lucy Raymond, a purveyor of farm-fresh eggs and milk, was quite a sly businesswoman. If her hens weren't laying, she would "borrow" eggs from a store in Stamford and sell them as her own. When the pasteurization laws came into effect and it was no longer legal to sell raw milk, she left a large milk can on her porch, along with a can for "donations."

The unknown writer mentioned "The Homestead," the home of James A. Wakeman, a prominent Lewisboro farmer. The Wakemans have a road named after them and there are still Wakemans living in Vista. The Homestead is now called Wakeman Farm.

After crossing a bridge over a "small stream of water" flowing like Tennyson's "brook," we come to Lazelle Farm on the right-hand side of the road, owned by William C. Hanford. The Hanfords were also prominent members of the community. Continuing north, before reaching Shady Lane, the Charles Raymond farm, which stretches alongside both sides of Elmwood Avenue as far as Onatru Farm, comes into view. "The Homestead, where Charles A. Raymond and all his children were born, is one of the particularly pleasant places." This home, for many years, belonged to the Deiches family. It rests on the left-hand side of Elmwood Avenue.

Shortly thereafter is "a romantic drive on a cross street known as 'Shady Lane' crossing to the parallel road." Then Onatru Farm appears on the right-hand side. Onatru Farm belonged to E.V.Z. Lane of New York. The writer said, "Mr. Lane has a large interest in the Mapes Fertilizing Co. He spends two or three months during the season on the farm." E.V.Z. Lane was the father of Alice Lane Poor. Mrs. Poor inherited the one-hundred-acre farm from her parents and donated portions of it to the town in the 1970s.

Next on the route are the two Ketcham places, also on the right-hand side of the street, and occupied only during the summer. "They command a sightly prospect toward Long Island Sound," declares our unknown tour guide. At the end of the avenue, at the north fork in the road, is the home of Henry Olmstead. This delightful Connecticut saltbox has belonged to the Armistead family since the early 1940s. Ms. Karen Armistead is a master gardener and has kept up her showplace gardens throughout the years.

To the east, on the Ridgefield Road (West Lane) "are the spacious grounds and fine buildings on either side of the street belonging to Dr. George G. Shelton." Dr. Shelton led the Lewisboro Association's campaign to do away with "buying votes" in local elections, a common practice in farm country that prevailed in turn-of-the-century Lewisboro. And there ends our drive along the elm tree–lined avenue, still a very pleasant trip.

Originally published on August 23, 2001.
(Note: Karen Armistead died in March 2006.)

Vista Woods

Vista residents of a certain age remember with a faint shudder the cluster of unpainted, dilapidated houses lining the west side of Smithridge Road where Oakridge Commons is now. Originally envisioned as a neighborhood with at least three streets arranged in a square-block pattern, including Bryon Road, Ruscoe Road and Adelmer Street, and fronting on Vista Avenue (Smithridge Road), the plans looked admirable on paper. Plans for this development (to be called Vista Woods) were submitted to the Lewisboro Building Department in September 1941, shortly before the country became involved in World War II. Eva C. Bryon of Saugerties, New York, was owner of the property and development company. Bryon was the second wife of Dr. Benn Adelmar (sometimes Adelmer) Bryon of Ridgefield.

A respected doctor, who practiced medicine in Ridgefield and later in New Canaan, Bryon served the Connecticut and New York communities well for more than fifty years. According to Ridgefield historian Richard Venus, Dr. Bryon was called Barney by most people, but not out of disrespect: "[T]he name was derived from the rapid manner in which he drove his auto" and reminded people of Barney Oldfield, a famous race car driver of the era.

Wishing to supplement his physician's income, Dr. Bryon apparently went into the real estate business, developing a section of Ridgefield off High Ridge Avenue (surrounding St. Mary's Church) that is still known as Bryon Park. It is a neighborhood of friendly looking homes. Mr. Venus called Barney Bryon "a man of vision and the town is better off because of his efforts." The Bryon family lived in a large Victorian house, where the erstwhile Grand Union operated until about a year ago. The home was demolished and the property's beautiful elm trees were eventually cut down to make way for the store's parking lot.

Long before the Vista debacle, the good doctor had begun the development of the Lake Kitchawan area in the 1920s (later Kitchawan Park). That development certainly fared better than what he was involved in during the early 1940s.

Dr. Bryon was well-known in Lewisboro as a physician and had many patients. How patients thought of him, in this respect, is not on the record. However, anyone who ever had to live with the sight of the houses erected by his development company along Vista Avenue (as Route 123/Smithridge Road was called then) had nothing favorable to tell. The structures built during the early forties were a blight on the area, by all accounts.

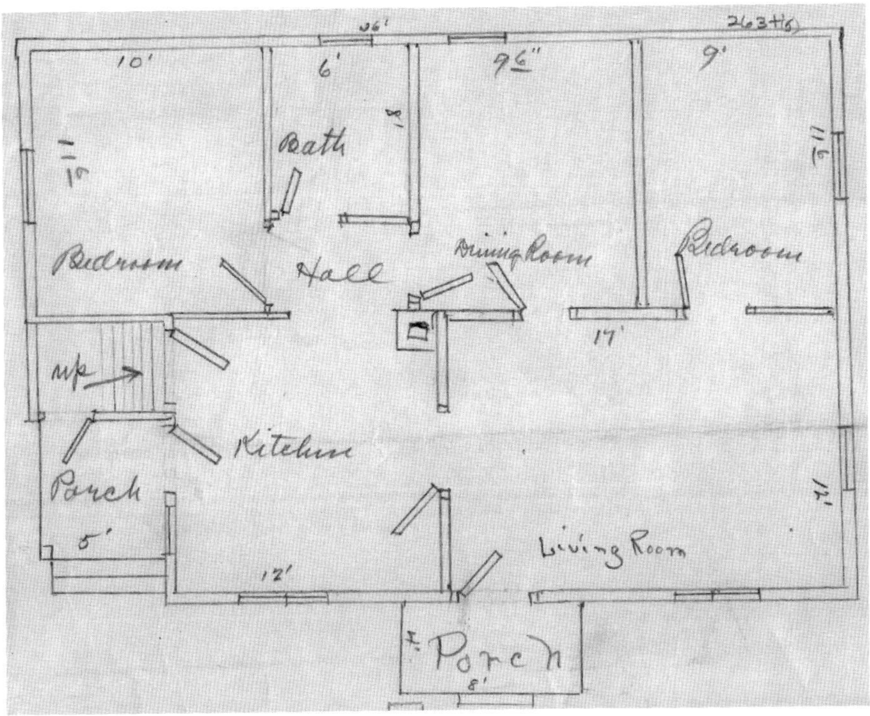

This is a sketch of a Vista Woods floor plan for a one-story house from the files of the Lewisboro Building Department.

In an article published in the *Lewisboro Ledger* in May 1977, Editor Chris Noblet related a local story that the good doctor really wanted to build a service station but was denied. He decided to thumb his nose at the town fathers and build some shoddy houses instead. Building permits exist for six houses that were built over a period of several years. Perhaps it was the wartime economy or just ill will on the part of Dr. Bryon, but residents who remember them say the houses were never properly finished on the outside. They were shingled or sided, but not painted. In the 1950s, locals described the area, and not with fondness, as looking like a Tobacco Road.

Mr. Noblet quoted longtime resident Mrs. Roslyn Peck, who watched as the houses were built and also as they were demolished twenty-five years later. "The houses were right up against the road so you could barely get a car in front," Mrs. Peck said in the article. "They painted the houses up and put on imitation siding. It looked like shingles, but it was tar paper!"

In Mr. Noblet's article, Vista residents of the time described the Vista Woods homeowners as "sort of loners who didn't even mingle with each other too much, although a mixed bag of people, they were 'okay,' though."

In my recent conversations, old-time residents described the houses as "deplorable." Everyone I talked with remembered the collections of derelict cars and household detritus littering the yards—bathtubs, iceboxes, sinks and just "stuff" that never seemed to go anywhere. There were no lawns or attempts to landscape the yards.

A blueprint and building plans in my files show plans for six houses with footprints between 22' x 22' and 36' x 30'—dimensions less than small houses by today's standards set by mini- and maxi-mansions. Lot sizes ranged from 100' x 125' to 100' x 108'. All structures were described as two-story, one-family residences and the estimated building cost per structure was $2,000.

By the early 1960s, Vista Woods had seen its day. The New Canaan Development Company had been acquiring properties in the surrounding area for several years, and in January 1961, it began applying for demolition permits to prepare the way for a shopping center. The New Canaan Development Company gave way to the Oakridge Land and Development Corporation, which continued the demolition process and led, finally, to the

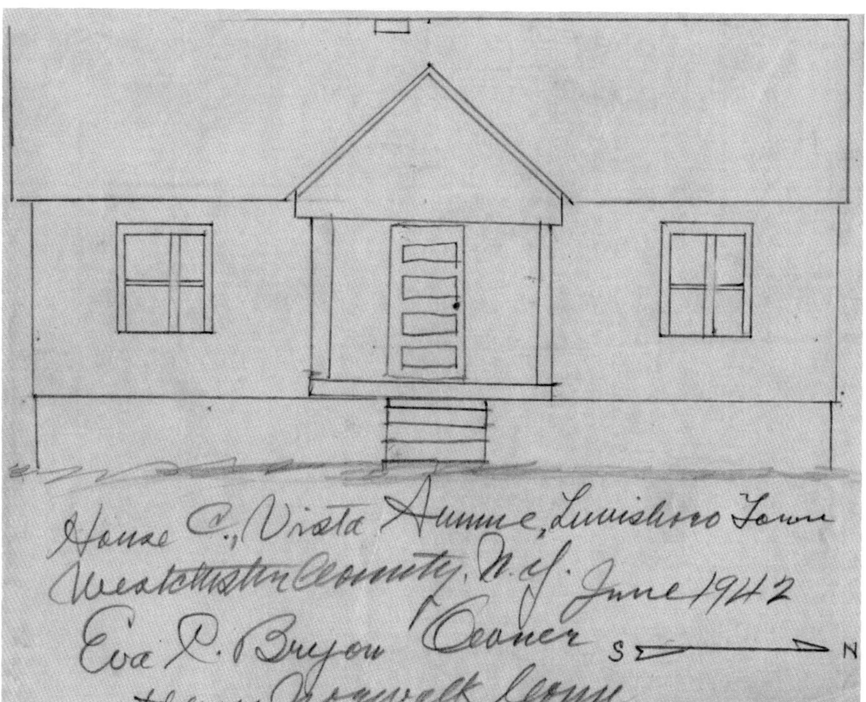

This exterior view of a Vista Woods one-story house didn't match the shabby appearance of the houses that were built by Dr. Bryon.

end of Tobacco Road. Oakridge Condominiums and Oakridge Commons Center, familiar to all who travel Smithridge Road today, are the results.

Dr. B. Adelmar Bryon died December 23, 1949, after a long illness. He was survived by his second wife, Eva Hill Bryon; a son, the Reverend Adelmar Bryon; and a daughter, Kathryn Bryon (both children of his first wife, Vera). Not wanting to speak ill of the deceased, one Lewisboro resident remembered her young adulthood in the hamlet. She whispered that, as she understood it, Dr. Bryon was involved in many things, and in her mind, he was not always a "person of ethics." It is rather sad that a doctor who was so respected by his patients and remembered for the things he accomplished in other places is looked on as such a dishonorable gentleman in Lewisboro, especially in Vista.

Originally published on February 7, 2002.

Sterns Were Spies After All, or So It Seems

With all the talk about spies nowadays, we can't let this opportunity go by without mentioning the role that Lewisboro has played in the games of foreign intrigue and espionage over the centuries. Where are you, James Bond and John le Carré?

First we played jailor to Major John André, co-conspirator with the master turncoat of them all, General Benedict Arnold. Arnold handed over the plans of West Point to Major André, who was subsequently captured and brought to Major Sheldon's headquarters on Main Street in South Salem, where he spent the better part of two days in September 1780. While being held prisoner in South Salem, the handsome, popular and talented André wrote to George Washington, explaining who he was and asking to be treated as an officer rather than a spy, a request Washington was forced to deny. In the end, André got the gibbet while Arnold escaped to freedom and a new life in England.

Following the Revolutionary War, Goldens Bridge was home for a time to Enoch Crosby, the inspiration for Harvey Birch in James Fenimore Cooper's *The Spy*. The character of Birch was based on the espionage exploits of Crosby, who traveled throughout Putnam and Westchester Counties, gathering information about the British for spymaster George Washington (who often ran his own spies, not trusting the task to others).

Fast-forwarding to the 1940s and 1950s, we come to another wartime era in Lewisboro—the cold war. Our town saw a lot of patriotic activity during World War II. We had civil defense patrols, scrap collections, war bond sales and the South Salem Studios. Enzo Yocca's South Salem Studios produced scale models of warships and planes (used for training purposes) for the Department of the Navy and other branches of the military.

Lewisboro residents also heard whispers of spies in their midst, in the wilds of Lewisboro hamlet. Some of these whispers probably had substance, at least if they involved the Sterns. The family lived in a charming old home on Kitchawan Road. They lived in town slightly more than a decade, from the early 1940s to 1953, when they left town quietly and quickly. But we are getting ahead of the story.

This spy story is about the glamorous and amorous daughter of a Southern diplomat and her rich Midwestern husband, both of whom, like many other idealists of this era, believed or dabbled in the philosophies of the Communist Party. Alfred Stern was chairman of the Illinois Housing Commission in the 1930s and was a major contributor to the German Communist Party. He also founded the Institute for Psychoanalysis in Chicago.

Martha Dodd, the daughter of William Edward Dodd of Clayton, North Carolina, was born in 1908, in Ashland, Virginia. Her father was a noted historian—a professor of history at the University of Chicago and Randolph-Macon College. Chosen by his good friend Franklin Delano Roosevelt to be America's ambassador to Germany in 1933, he took his family along. The Dodd family remained in Berlin until Ambassador Dodd was recalled in 1937. He was strongly anti-Nazi, as was his vivacious daughter (for the most part).

While in Berlin, rumor has it that Martha fell in love with the dashing Boris Vinogradov, a Soviet diplomat stationed there. KGB files recently opened to the public contained love letters from Martha to Boris and a note wherein she offered to become a Soviet operative and do anything in her capacity as the daughter of the American ambassador to further the Soviet cause. A small excerpt proclaimed "that my services of any kind and at any time are proposed to the party for use at its discretion."

Martha was in her late twenties at the time of the offer. The KGB files indicated that she had romantic liaisons with a selection of diplomats, newspapermen and Nazi officials during her five years in the German capital, but she truly loved Boris and wanted to marry him, if "Uncle Joe" Stalin would permit it. Instead, Uncle Joe permitted the persecution of

This house on Mill River Road once belonged to Arthur and Martha Stern, who were accused of being Soviet spies by the U.S. government.

Vinogradov, who was eliminated in one of the Soviet purges, a fact Martha did not learn until after her marriage to Alfred Stern in 1938.

After graduating from the University of Chicago, Martha worked as an assistant literary editor at the *Chicago Tribune*. During her stay in Germany, she wrote a book column in a newspaper for English-speaking expatriates. After her return to the United States, she edited her father's Berlin diaries and published several books, including *Through Embassy Eyes*, an account of her Berlin adventures.

Martha's spying, however, was pretty much limited to opening her father's mail and reporting on the gossip heard at embassy gatherings. She did offer to persuade her father to have FDR appoint a Soviet sympathizer as his replacement as ambassador to Berlin. The offer went unanswered.

Martha Dodd was called "comely and capricious, a courtesan, agent and student of communism under her father's eyes."

Upon her return to the United States and her marriage to Alfred Stern, she continued her marginal espionage activities and, in 1942, recruited her husband to join her in the fun. In 1943, according to an indictment handed

This postcard from the Sterns was sent to Elisha Keeler in 1952 during one of their "vacations."

down in 1957, Boris Morros, a flamboyant Hollywood musical director for Paramount Studios and a Soviet agent since 1934, was asked to cooperate with the Sterns and was brought to the Kitchawan Road home by a Russian diplomat from Washington, D.C.

A music publishing company was set up, financed by Alfred Stern, to provide a front for Morros's spying activities, and as a cover for his agents who traveled throughout Europe. Boris Morros was the longest-serving Soviet agent, serving from 1934 until 1957, when he confessed all to the United States government, implicating the Sterns in the process. Morros's cover name was Frost. Martha was known as Liza.

For several years, the Sterns' money sustained the Morros music company front, but Boris Morros was an incompetent business manager and managed to lose $130,000 of Alfred's money. The two also had a falling out over the publishing of the hit song, "The Chattanooga Choo Choo." Relations between the spies were strained to say the least.

Alfred and Martha were members of the Communist Party of the United States of America, and it is rumored, but not substantiated, that they were friendly with former Vice President Henry Wallace, owner of Farvue Farm in South Salem, and helped convince him to accept Communist Party backing during his bid for president in 1948.

The 1957 espionage indictment handed down, in absentia, accused the couple of "conspiracy to transmit military and political information to the Soviets." Knowing that the jig was up, the Sterns had begun taking extended vacations about 1952, and quietly fled the country in 1953, defecting to Mexico City. When deportation loomed in 1957, the Sterns took on Paraguayan citizenship and fled to Prague. In 1963, they set up a residence in Cuba, where they remained until 1970. Eventually, they landed back in Prague, where they spent the rest of their lives in a dream gone awry.

In 1979, after spying charges were dropped by the U.S. government because of a lack of available witnesses (everyone had died), Martha and Alfred Stern petitioned President Jimmy Carter for a pardon so they could return to their homeland, but the request was either denied or ignored. Alfred Stern died in Prague in 1986, at the age of eighty-eight. In 1990, Martha Dodd Stern died at the age of eighty-two, also in Prague.

Elisha Keeler, formerly of South Salem and Lehigh Acres, Florida, was a part-time caretaker for the Sterns at their Kitchawan estate. Mr. Keeler said he only saw Martha Stern in the afternoon, when she would come out and chat with him. He described her as an attractive and pleasant woman "who always seemed to be most busy in the evenings. She never made an appearance before noon, when she took her breakfast," he reported in a telephone conversation.

Mr. Keeler was contacted by the FBI during the early 1950s and asked to keep an eye out for known Soviet operatives who might be visitors at the home of the Sterns. He was given a collection of FBI mug shots to study, but he claims he never saw any of the "spies" while he was in the Stern's employ. Elisha Keeler says he doesn't know if the rumors about the Sterns were true or not. In his opinion, they were pleasant people, as was their houseboy, Ralph, who took care of their son, Robert. The only strange thing about them, in his mind, was the hours that they kept! And the secrets they took to their graves.

Originally published on March 8, 2001.
(Note: Elisha Keeler died in 2005, at the age of ninety-eight.)

Part III

South Salem

So Whose Bones Were They?

Tradition has it that William Truesdale and Samuel Tuttle were "likely candidates as the first settlers of Lewisboro," according to Jordan and Koehl's *History of the Town of Lewisboro*. The land that is now South Salem was included in the Ridgefield Proprietors' purchase from the local Indians. Truesdale and Tuttle were given a patent or deed to the land about 1728. At this time, the two speculators petitioned the Ridgefield landholders: "We being gotten upon said land have been at considerable charge to remove our families and labor done on said lands and desire that you account us equal sharers." The petition was granted. The story goes that shortly after that, William Truesdale was killed by Indians and his bones were found on the hillside that is now called Truesdale Hill. This area is probably the hilly region between Main Street and Truesdale Lake, near the intersection of Bouton Road and Main Street. There is no further mention of Mr. Tuttle anywhere.

What a great pioneering story—an early settler killed by Indians as he protected his wife, family and log cabin in the wilderness that was Salem in the 1700s. And that is the tale I always tell whenever I speak about the early days of our town. However, information has come to light that makes this story a little questionable, as colorful as it is.

While researching another family, the Tylers, I came across certain Truesdale (or Truesdell) information that blew the Indian story away. There was a William Truesdell (according to the reference I was using, Truesdale is the British spelling, and Truesdell is the American spelling), who was born April 6, 1700, in Dedham, Massachusetts. He married Martha Tyler of Branford, Connecticut, on April 21, 1719. William and Martha Truesdale had eleven children and the last was born in 1744.

According to the book *Our Rich Family* by Duane Wilson, his ancestor, William Truesdell, "lived in Branford, Norwalk and in the Oblong [South Salem and Vista area] and had a strong penchant for enterprise with interesting, but sometimes, unpleasant results." The Truesdell information tells of several run-ins with the courts for fraudulent land deals and nasty business betrayals for which William was imprisoned; he was bailed out by

Truesdale Lake, named for the hapless William Truesdale, was designed to be a vacation wonderland with private beaches, tennis and golf for its residents.

his father-in-law, John Tyler, in 1732. The article states that he made his living as a tanner, miller and land agent. In 1728 (note the date), he bought one hundred acres in Westchester County on speculation for £50. That land was sold for £350 in 1729.

William was jailed again, in October 1732, for fraudulent business dealings (probably a setup by his boss, Francis Harrison, who was a major land speculator in lower Westchester County). This time he served nine weeks in prison, and during that time he lost most of his earthly possessions, including his silver belt buckle and his clothing! Meanwhile, creditors took everything in his Connecticut home, sold the property and left his wife and six small children destitute. Given the date and the unreliability of the boundaries at the time, the home could have been in the Oblong territory (i.e. South Salem). He was able to recover much of the lost property and his belongings when he got out of prison. Considering these facts, maybe Mrs. Truesdell made up the Indian story herself!

Sometime before 1751, William moved to New Jersey with his son, Stephen. William died in Great Egg Harbor, Atlantic County, New Jersey, on September 21, 1751. William's will listed his assets as totaling twenty-four pounds. Martha is not mentioned in the document and Mary was the only child mentioned by name. Perhaps Martha died before the move to New Jersey. A son, Jesse, born in 1734, was mentioned in the will as having owned a house near Lake Truesdale. That house was still standing in the 1950s. Jesse died in North Salem in 1817.

That is the *new* legend of William Truesdale for whom one of our prettiest lakes is named. Perhaps someone can set it to music and tell it around summer lakeside campfires. Let me know if you do!

Originally published on March 1, 2006.

Upstairs, Downstairs in the Lawrence Household

The old, brown, suede-covered daybook of Cyrus Lawrence, Esq., never ceases to amaze. It sparks an interest in nineteenth-century life in South Salem. Cyrus's gravestone in the South Salem Cemetery tells us that he was born in 1827 and died in 1897. He spent about thirty of those years as the leading merchant of South Salem. His store was located where the Textile Conservation Workshop now stands on Main Street, just a couple of doors down from the White Church.

Cyrus Lawrence was one of the lovable characters from our town's past. He was the village merchant from 1861 until his death. He also served as the postmaster. The post office was located in his general store and the mail was delivered twice daily. Mr. Lawrence was elected justice of the peace in 1867 and also held that office until his death. He was known to be a very fair man and was well liked and respected by all the townsfolk.

His daybook offers a unique glimpse into his day-to-day business operations and the family household workings. We invite the reader to journey back a little more than a century to the times of Cyrus Lawrence. Our first glance is at a time just after the Civil War—December 1867.

Mr. Lawrence noted the following in his daybook: "Ellen Thomas Gribble of Birmingham, England. Dec. 6th, 1867—commenced work for indefinite time, to be paid what her services are worth. (No price agreed)."

He then noted cash paid out in her behalf: "To cash paid at boardinghouse in New York (Pier #3)—$2.50; paid for carrying trunk—$.50; fair on railroad to Katonah—$1.30."

Not only did Cyrus pay for this lady's journey to his South Salem home, but he also provided a suitable wardrobe for life in the country. "Jan. 1868—2 yds Calico—$.25; Paid Caleb Burt for shoes—$3.50; 2 1/2 yds calico—$.31, etc."

By April, things apparently had not worked out and Mrs. Ellen Gribble left the employ of the Lawrences and returned to New York City. On April 6, there is a notation that states, "by 4 months work—1 at $3 and 3 at $5 equals $18, minus $10.60 for sundries, etc." The woman received the grand total of $7.40, plus an extra $0.25 he threw in for good measure. On April 8, she "left for New York."

There were other brief descriptions of girls or women in their service, none of whom seemed to last more than a couple of months at a time. One young girl, possibly the daughter of a Frank Miller, was hired in May 1868. This poor specimen lasted nine weeks before she "ran away from service and did not return (Good!)." From her $9.50 wages, he deducted $3.26 for "stove, crockery and other things lost, destroyed or broken by her."

The next backward glance takes us to May 1873. That's the day Miss Hannah Elizabeth Waters, eleven years old, "came here on trial to hire until she is 18 years old if she suits and a satisfactory bargain can be made." Things started out just fine. The Lawrences supplied her with:

Two pair of shoes bot [sic] *of H. Smith—$2.00; a new calico dress—$2.00; 2 calico dresses (buttons)—$2.50; 2 aprons—$.38; 5 yds. Black muslin for underclothes—$1.00; 1 Hat trimmings—$3.00; pr. Stockings—$.30; Gray suit dress and sack—$3.00; pr. Gloves—$.40; Ribbons for sash—$1.40; Ribbons for hair, pink and blue—$.80.*

The last entry for Hannah appeared on December 29, 1874: "Went home not to return again. Was not satisfactory and did not suit us." We wonder just what duties Miss Hannah Waters performed that did not suit the affable Mr. Lawrence, and how life turned out for the young lady after her sojourn in the Lawrence household.

Good servants may have been hard to come by, but life meandered on, through good times and bad, through sickness and health. Our ancestors had myriad remedies to combat the ills that still plague us. I found a few receipts in the daybook that I'd like to pass along for whatever they're worth.

I am not sure if the first receipt is for humans or horses since it appears smack in the middle of the veterinary complaints. Except for the turpentine, the ingredients seem almost palatable: "For Enlarged or Thick Glands—1 pint vinegar, 1 pint turpentine, 1 fresh egg and Tablespoon honey." I would advise smearing this concoction externally!

Here is an "excellent remedy for cholera, cholera morbus, dysentery, diarrhea, cramps in stomach, etc. Dose: From 15 drops to a teaspoonful. Mixed with a little water and sweetened with sugar. Give as often as the case requires." It is dated September 1862. Here's the receipt:

Laudanum: 1¼ oz
Essence of Peppermint: 1¼ oz.
Tincture of rhubarb: 1¼ oz.
Tincture of cayenne pepper: 1¼ oz.
Camphor: 2 Drachmas

I doubt if that remedy would get FDA approval nowadays.

How about Dr. Breakell's remedy for coughs? Dr. James Breakell lived in Cross River. He was elected town supervisor in 1892 and served for one year. He was the last supervisor to do so since the term of office was changed to two years after his tenure. He was not reelected, much to the pleasure of the town's "old guard," who considered him an out-of-towner since he was not native to Lewisboro.

The mansard-roofed home of Cyrus Lawrence, overlooking South Salem's main intersection, is as impressive today as it was in 1872, the year it was built.

Gather the following ingredients to make one heck of a cough syrup!

2 oz. solid extract belladonna
2 oz. powdered black licorice
2 oz. powdered [illegible] *potash*
1 pint strained honey

Place a walnut-sized lump, twice a day, on back of mouth or on back teeth.

An alternative remedy, judged effective by Cyrus, was Professor Reynolds's remedy for coughs. Try it. You'll like it, and it just might work: "Bicarbonate of soda and half as much saltpeter and half as much alum as saltpeter. Teaspoonful twice a day for a few days, then once a day."

Cyrus Lawrence wrote, "Each of these remedies are claimed to be much used in New York City and to be infallible."

Originally published on December 5, 2004.

Number, Please!

Part of what makes the position of town historian so interesting is the people one meets in the course of pursuing Lewisboro's history. One of the most knowledgeable and interesting men I ever had the chance to meet was the late Oliver Knapp of Mount Kisco. "Ollie" Knapp knew more about Mount Kisco and other parts of northern Westchester County than any ten others put together. He was the Mount Kisco town historian for many years, and he was also very knowledgeable about the history of the telephone company in our part of the county. I believe he worked for the New York Telephone Company for about fifty years.

Ollie knew a lot about Lewisboro in the early years of the twentieth century, too. On his mother's side, he was related to the Todds. He was very familiar with the Todd Road area of our town and he spent several afternoons guiding me around town. As I drove, he spoke into my tape recorder in his lap, expounding on the history so dear to him. He also filled me in on some of the history of telephone service in Lewisboro. Ollie told me he installed the first telephones at Farvue Farm for Vice President Henry A. Wallace in the mid-1940s. He then came back twenty years later and converted those old-fashioned phones to dial phones when dials were introduced to Lewisboro in the early 1960s. But we are getting way ahead of the story.

Alexander Graham Bell may have invented the telephone in 1876, but it was about twenty years later that Lewisboro got its first telephone. We don't know how many telephone machines were installed at that time, but two instances are noted in *History of the Town of Lewisboro*. One was in Vista, at the home of Ed Ruscoe who lived behind the Vista Market. His phone was installed on the Norwalk-to-Ridgefield line. Meanwhile, Cyrus Lawrence's general store in South Salem boasted a telephone as well, installed in that same year. Mr. Lawrence's telephone was hooked into the Ridgefield line—probably no relation to the Norwalk line mentioned above. In 1907, another line was run from Katonah to the village of South Salem—the Hudson River Company's line. Connecticut lines could not hook into New York lines, which caused a huge problem when the companies tried to set up a party line about 1900. It seems that if you wanted to talk east, you used the telephone on the Ridgefield line; if your party was in Katonah, you used the Hudson River Company instrument and wires. Sound confusing? Well, it was.

In 1912, the New York Telephone Company began to absorb all the smaller independent lines and Ma Bell was on her way.

In 1983, Oliver Knapp wrote a one-page history of South Salem's beloved Lawrence telephone exchange. We'll quote from him:

> *In 1911, John Lawrence, who maintained a farm on Spring Street and Main Streets, allowed the New York Telephone Company to install a single position switchboard on the second floor of his farm house. Adjacent to the small switchboard room was a bedroom that the night operator occupied when the telephone traffic permitted, during which time a night bell alerted the operator to incoming calls.*

Louisa Tinè, the present owner of the Lawrence farmhouse, described the switchboard room in a telephone interview (how appropriate!) recently. Mrs. Tinè said the room was beautifully paneled with oak and contained a large oak desk and a huge wooden cabinet for the switchboard connections and telephone lines. The former switchboard room is located on the second floor in the rear of the house. A section of the house that included the historic telephone exchange was badly damaged by fire while the family was away on Christmas Night 1982. During the reconstruction of the house, the desk was removed but Mr. Knapp convinced the owners that the historic switchboard cabinet should remain in place. "We keep books in it now," Mrs. Tinè said. The night operator's bedroom is used as a guest bedroom by the family.

From 1911 until December 19, 1939, the upstairs "turn-the-crank" telephone exchange provided all of the area's telephone service. At first, John Lawrence's older daughter Marion operated the exchange. Later on, her sister Elizabeth took over and divided her time between chores (making and selling butter, cheese, milk and eggs with her sister-in-law, Mary Lawrence) and running the telephone exchange. Mary Lawrence taught many of the older generation of townsfolk, first in the one-room schoolhouse in the village, and then at Lewisboro School. Elizabeth never married, but as the local switchboard operator, she was the social center of the village, privy to many of the ins and outs of the illnesses, trials and triumphs of townsfolk.

According to Mr. Knapp's notes, some telephone subscribers advised Elizabeth Lawrence of their whereabouts if they were not going to be at home for any length of time. She would take their messages for them and present them to the patrons upon their return.

In a small town, it's only right that everyone knows about everyone else's business. That was made even easier by the party-line system that was finally set up about 1912, after the aforementioned difficulty with a multitude of lines and companies had been resolved. The operator would ring the bell

The South Salem dial central office on Spring Street was put into service on December 19, 1939. No more "turn-the-crank" service!

code and a specific number of rings at each household would alert the home to an incoming call and put the call through. Listening in on others' conversations was not beyond the nosy parkers of the community! Everyone knew which number of rings was specific to which family.

Thus went the telephone service until the modern era in 1939, when the turn-the-crank system was replaced by the new dial system. The telephone company built a brand-new brick building on the corner of the Lawrence farm, near the South Salem Cemetery on Spring Street, where it still stands today. It seems that millions of wires come into that little building where once a very simple system flourished. Those early phone numbers had only two digits. When we moved to town almost forty years ago, we only had to dial four digits to call another party with the same exchange. Even to call Ridgefield, Connecticut, one did not have to dial "1" to get out of the state. Sad was the day when the telephone company announced that we all had to dial seven digits to call the same friends we had been dialing only four digits to reach for so many years. That four-digit dialing system made us feel special and distinct from our city friends in lower Westchester. One can only imagine the immense change when the switch was made from the friendly voice of Elizabeth Lawrence to the annoying buzz of the dial tone. Progress is not always pretty.

Now, as we enter the twenty-first century, we are facing another revolution in telephone communication—cellphones. What would Elizabeth or Marion think? Would they be amazed at the ease and impersonal touch of today's phone system? Would they approve of cell towers located along our

The switchboard in this picture was similar to the one used by the Lawrence sisters in their farmhouse until 1939, when the dial phone made its appearance.

highways? Or would the forward-thinking John Lawrence erect a cell tower right on Echo Farm, in his very own backyard?

Originally published on January 17, 2003.

Jamie Remembered

November heralds the onset of the darker days of autumn—the sun sets with a golden glow and the wind brings with it a rustle of leaves and sometimes a cold rain. It also gives us time to remember loved ones no longer among us, whether that time occurs via All Souls' Day or, in a more secular way, Veterans Day. In remembrance of our servicemen and women who have fought in all the wars that have gone before, and those presently defending our honor and democracy abroad, I want to devote this space to a young man whose small memorial sits atop the little knoll at the corner of Spring Street and Route 35 in South Salem. Looking back at the event that the memorial honors, perhaps it defines the start of today's world of terrorism, color codes of danger and threats to our peaceful coexistence with our fellow man. The memorial was erected in 1988 and reads:

They Came in Peace—
Dedicated to the Loving Memory of
CPL James Journay Jackowski, USMC,
South Salem, Lewisboro
And his fellow peacekeepers killed in the Terrorist Bombing
of the Marine Corps Headquarters
in Beirut, Lebanon
on October 23, 1983.
Lest We Forget that Peace has a Price.

In this twenty-third anniversary year of that tragic event, I would like to repeat sections of my "Window on Spring Street" column from the November 16, 1983 *Ledger*. The interview with Jamie's mother, Mary Ellen Jackowski, conducted just a couple of weeks after her son's death, was the most difficult I have ever done.

I never knew Jamie Jackowski. Over the years, I'd heard his mother talk about him and several years ago I featured him in this column, but I never had an opportunity to meet him. Now I'll never have the chance, except through the loving and courageous eyes of his parents, their photo albums and Jamie's letters. Jamie was one of the 241 servicemen killed in Beirut, Lebanon, on Sunday, October 23—a cold, dank day here in South Salem and a gloomy day for the whole nation.

U.S. involvement in Lebanon was so far away from us all. Then one day the reality of it was brought home to our town. It was brought home in a box, draped with an American flag. The flag, the dog tags and the memories are all that is left of a boy's life—a life that should be hopes and dreams and promises, not just memories for those who stand bewildered, holding the mementos, the flag and the dog tags.

Jamie Jackowski was born on July 19, 1963. The Jackowski family moved to South Salem about six years ago. Jamie attended John Jay High School, where he participated in cross-country for two years. Throughout his high school career and, in fact, several years before that, Jamie had indicated a strong interest in the culinary arts. As a special treat for when he graduated from the eighth grade in Sloatsburg, his parents took him to dinner at the Culinary Institute of America in Hyde Park.

While at John Jay, Jamie was very active in the Home Economics Department, winning several awards, including the 1980 "Super Chef Award," represented by a huge white chef's hat. In 1979, he received a Certificate of Excellence in Service from the department.

Mrs. Jackowski fondly remembers the mutual admiration enjoyed by her son and home economics teacher Liz Berman. Mrs. Berman shared Jamie's love of life and enthusiasm and Jamie remembered her birthday by bringing her flowers.

His high school teachers remembered him, and several attended Jamie's funeral, which was gratifying to his mother. Mary Ellen Jackowski noted, "The teachers who came to the church and who were at the wake were the ones who meant the most to Jamie. I'm so glad they are the ones who Jamie made a lasting impression on. These were the teachers he cared about, and they were the ones who cared about him."

Jamie's desire to follow a culinary career led him to join the U.S. Marines during his senior year in high school. He completed his high school education in the Marine Corps and was planning to attend college when he was discharged. He received high marks on his entrance exams, which assured him his chosen field (cooking, of course). An army travels on its stomach and the Marine Corps is no exception. A cook's role is a crucial one. When asked what he would like to eat after returning from a cruise aboard the USS *Nassau*, Jamie informed his mother in no uncertain terms, "No rabbit or lobster, please!" Fortunately, Mrs. Jackowski said that neither item was in her menu plans, although she was never certain of the reasons for his request.

Corporal James Jackowski was a fun-loving, warm-hearted human being. He was easygoing, but at the same time, he was sensitive to other people's feelings and thoughts. Even though he was the youngest child in the family, Jamie knew how to play the role of big brother for the neighborhood children and his younger cousins. "He was a tough Marine who always remembered my love for cats," said Mrs. Jackowski with a smile. "He always had a feline-type souvenir for me when he returned from a cruise."

Jamie left behind a black-and-white cat when he enlisted. He had found his scrawny little "Loco" abandoned near the New York Thruway on his way to school one day, and his junior high school teachers nourished and cared for the cat all day until he could ask his parents' permission to keep it. Mrs. Jackowski said she worried that something would happen to Loco before Jamie returned from the Marine Corps.

Jamie was an avid skier. The family often skied together. He loved being outdoors, and during his sixteenth summer, he worked in the Youth Conservation Corps, an organization funded by Westchester County that employed youths (ages fifteen and up). Members of the corps worked in county parks tending animals, clearing paths and making trails. Jamie worked at Muscoot Farm Park and Teatown Reservation.

True to his heart's desires, Corporal Jackowski had worked in the deli section at Foodtown (now D'Agostinos) and at Alexander's Restaurant (formerly the Hayloft) in South Salem while he was in school.

Never one to apply himself strictly to his books, Jamie straightened out himself and his attitudes in basic training, said his mother. "The Marine Corps was good for him. His ideals seemed to have evolved. Things that weren't important to him before he went in suddenly were," she said.

Jamie had decided not to reenlist when his time was up because he had had enough and now he really knew what he wanted to do with his life. Mrs. Jackowski noted that in his last letter, "He seemed to have come to grips with the future. He was planning to return home and begin college to study cooking. He had already been accepted at the college of his choice in Sullivan County."

"Jamie touched a lot of people, and he doesn't even know it," Mary Ellen Jackowski concluded, sadly. "Wouldn't it be wonderful if we could share our feelings with each other more often?"

Encouragement, praise and love are meant to be given away, but items like these are probably the hardest gifts to give. A senseless loss of life for a young marine teaches us this lesson. John and Mary Ellen Jackowski, like their brave son, possess remarkable strength, courage and fortitude. They are able to give a smile or a hand to another in their shared grief. Somehow, when we most need it, God is there to supply these gifts of the Spirit.

Jamie is survived by his parents, a brother, John J. Jackowski Jr., a sister, Jacklyn J. Seguerra, and grandparents Stanley and Ruth Jackowski and Helen and Arthur McCartney.

A scholarship fund was set up in James J. Jackowski's name at John Jay High School. The award was to be given to a graduating senior who showed talent and interest in the culinary arts. The scholarship was given for a number of years. I do not know if it is still awarded.

The bronze plaque honoring the fallen servicemen was put in place at the Spring Street/Route 35 corner in 1989 and has stood sentinel along with two American flags ever since. We encourage you to visit the site and pause to reflect upon our freedom and its cost. Remember a brave young man who wanted to serve his country in the best way he knew how—to cook for his fellow marines.

In case you don't remember, tragedy struck the marine peacekeepers' headquarters in Beirut at 6:20 a.m. on October 23, 1983, when a suicide bomber drove his truck through security and into the lobby of the four-story building and detonated twelve thousand pounds of TNT. The explosion

The memorial dedicated to Corporal James Jackowski and the marines who lost their lives in the Beirut bombing graces the intersection of Spring Street and Route 35.

caused the structure to collapse, turning the building into rubble and a tomb for 220 marines stationed there as peacekeepers, 18 navy personnel and 3 soldiers. At least 60 American civilians were also injured.

Moments after the blast at the American compound, a truck was driven into the French quarters, killing fifty-eight paratroopers and wounding fifteen more. The world has never been the same.

Originally published on November 16, 1983, and republished on November 3, 2006.

A Christmas Tale of a Boy and His Tree

This is the tale of a special tree, a South Salem tree that had its fifteen minutes of fame. It is also the story of a man who loved his hometown of Lewisboro. That man was Wallace "Wally" Lawrence of South Salem. Wally was a man of many interests and a jack-of-all-trades. He was a preserver of history and a craftsman. A proud veteran of World War II, he was a paratrooper in the Eleventh Airborne Division, and saw action in the Philippines. Wallace Lawrence died in 1994, but his memory lives on among the older generation.

The Lawrence family played many parts in the development of the hamlet of South Salem. Lawrence farms, during the nineteenth century, occupied most of the land in the hamlet. Two of those properties, which were owned by Wally Lawrence's grandfather Elmer, are still recognizable today— Echo Farm on Spring Street and Sassafras Farm on Boway.

This story of a Christmas tree begins back during the Great Depression of the 1930s. Work was scarce, money was tight and people made do. Recycling was not the buzzword that it is today, but the townspeople of the mid-twentieth century had to recycle everything they could just to make ends meet in many cases. Collars and cuffs on work shirts were "turned" so the frayed edges wouldn't show, broken furniture became firewood to provide warmth in the winter and hand-me-downs were the rule in most families.

Wally's father, Gordon, was an architect and builder by training and would build a home that the family would live in until it sold, whereupon he would build another, and so it went during Wally's childhood. Two of these homes were on Lawrence property on Old Oscaleta Road, bordering the Connecticut line. The son was greatly influenced by his father's ingenuity and talents.

Born about one hundred years after the Lawrence family first came to South Salem, Wallace Lawrence grew up in a manner typical of a youngster in a farm community. He knew about cows and horses, hard work and education in a one-room school. Wally attended the North District School, better known as the Red Bridge Academy. He knew the tricks of the scholar—especially how to delay the opening of school on a cold winter's day by expertly allowing too much snow to accumulate in the stovepipe of the schoolroom's potbellied wonder. A wet, smoky fire did not make for a pleasant classroom!

Like all country boys, Wally Lawrence was familiar with the fields and woods in his vicinity. He often roamed the wooded sections of his family's property that bordered both sides of Main Street as it wandered its way toward Ridgefield. That's how Wally knew of a beautiful little tree hiding in the woods. The tree probably sprouted about the time Wally was born, growing as the boy did, with vigor and good faith in the future.

In 1937, as the country worked its way out of the Depression and toward prosperity once more, Gordon Lawrence built a house on Old Oscaleta Road. The home sat in the middle of a pasture, looking a bit barren—there was no extra money for landscaping. No matter, thought young Lawrence, now a strapping young man of twelve or thirteen. He knew where there was a lovely evergreen tree growing strong in the woods across Main Street. The tree was a Norway spruce, not really prolific in this neck of the woods, so to speak, but thriving just the same. With help, Wally dug the six-foot-tall tree and hauled it across the street and the meadow and planted it near the front door of the family's new house. Care was taken to see that the tree was watered and protected until it became rooted in its new home and grew into its responsibility to beautify the newly constructed house.

That Norway spruce grew and thrived for many decades, at least a generation. Wally grew up, married his sweetheart, Carolyn, and became the father of two daughters, Lynne and Alison. Following in the tradition of his father, Wally built a new home next door to the house with the Norway spruce and lived there with his family until his death. Meanwhile, he always had a notion that his little Norway spruce would make a perfect candidate for the Rockefeller Center Christmas tree. He mentioned this to his neighbors (the Eglers), who were now the owners of the tree. One early fall day in 1994, the Eglers announced to Wally that his lovely Norway spruce, now a majestic eighty feet tall, had been selected to grace the plaza

Wallace Lawrence enlisted in the U.S. Army after graduating from high school. He was very proud of his service during World War II.

at Rockefeller Center. Imagine the pleasure of that little boy in the past who had so carefully transplanted that spruce tree fifty-seven years ago. His dream was about to come true; the Norway spruce was scheduled to be cut down in early November.

As fate would have it, Wallace Lawrence, who suffered from lung cancer, would not live to see the tree cut down, wrapped and carefully lifted onto the truck for its fifty-mile ride to the Big Apple. He died on October 12, 1994. Ironically, on that day, the other members of his family were interviewed by the NBC *Today Show* about the story of the tree. The interviews took place in the morning and Wally passed away later that night, but at least he understood that his tree would make history as one of the very special ones, a beloved symbol to help New Yorkers celebrate the Christmas season. Not bad for a South Salem tree and a little boy with a shovel and a dream. Wallace Lawrence and that Norway spruce lived full lives and observed many changes in the town. The man and the tree, each in their own way, made the world a more pleasant place. With the help of Carolyn Lawrence, we can share this memory with you. Merry Christmas and holiday greetings to all.

Originally published in December 2006.

Part IV

Cross River

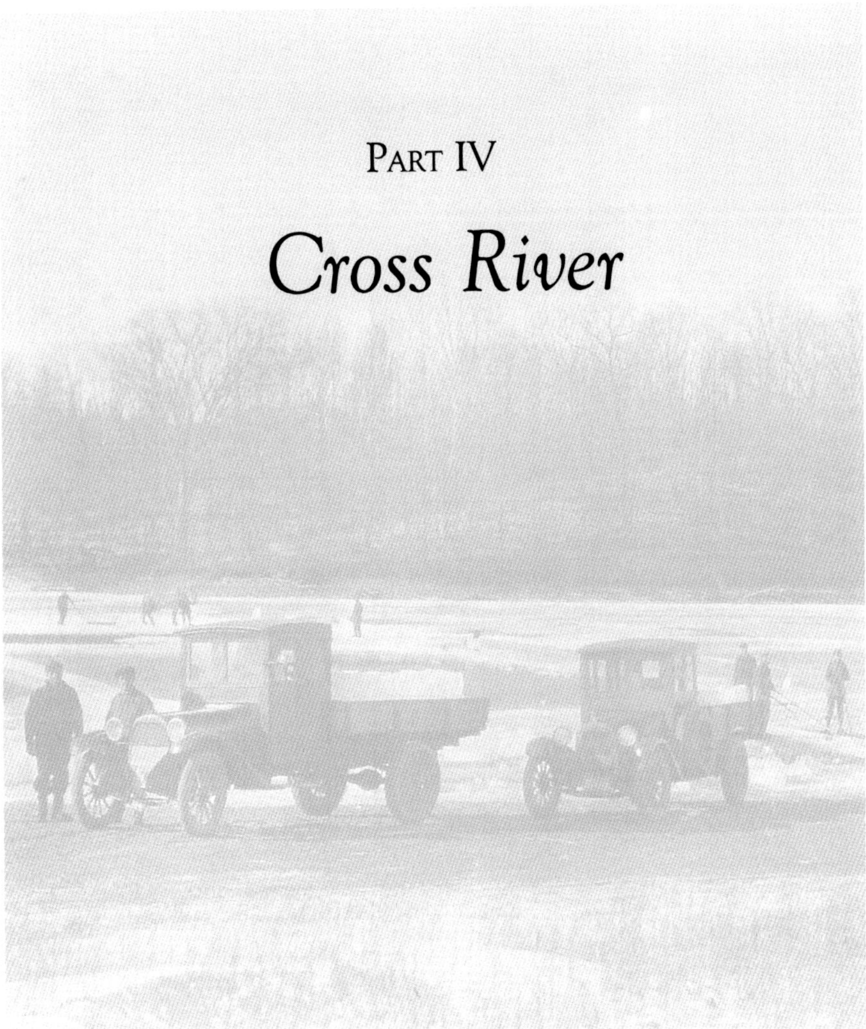

The Brick House

Gideon Reynolds's Brick House in Cross River on Route 121 still captures the imagination of travelers passing between Bedford and Cross River. Well over a century ago, it was a stagecoach stop and tavern, welcoming passengers on Gideon's postal conveyances between New York City and Danbury. In later years, the mansion was an inn, a summer tourist home, a tavern and a private residence.

The following poem was shared with us by Evelyn Russell of Cross River. Miss Russell is the daughter of Cyrus and Hazel Russell, and one of the few remaining direct descendants of the builder of the brick house that sits on the hill overlooking the reservoir. In 1829, when the house was constructed, it overlooked the village of Cross River and the river that flowed through the village. There was no reservoir. As the poem indicates, the bricks for the house were fired right on the property from local clay.

The poem was written by Geraldine F. Moore, Miss Russell's cousin. Mrs. Moore used the poem as the cover for her 2002 family Christmas calendar. It tells the old house's history quite succinctly.

There are some landmarks in history, which reach renown and fame,
While countless others stand apart, yet proud within their frame.
Knowing they have played a part in history's page as well,
Such is "the old Brick House," which has many tales to tell.
They built it many years ago, about eighteen twenty-nine,
A house of solid brick it is, they made it mighty fine.
The bricks were made right on the land, stacked in kilns and burned.
A slow laborious job it was, by many it was spurned.
The stage coach used to stop there, long long years ago,
When the pace of civilization was still a wee bit slow.
There were seventeen rooms within the house, and long and draughty halls

With twelve stone fireplaces to heat the old brick walls.
There's an R carved in the stone step, to denote the Reynolds name

The Brick House's parlor reflects a comfortable Victorian way of life on a sunny Cross River day.

Then the house passed down to Russells, the initial still the same.
Three generations were born there, Reynolds, Russell, Moore,
A house in Cross River history, which always will endure.
The family house and property was sold, about nineteen twenty-eight
And many different people have lived there since that date.
It's been a hostelry, a tavern, and now again an inn,
It changes with the wanderings of individual whim.
A stalwart it will always be, a landmark to tradition.
A reminder of the past—accomplishing its mission!

I would like to highlight a member of the last generation of Reynoldses born in the house—Evelyn Russell's father, Cyrus Russell.

As Miss Russell tells the story, her grandfather, William Harrison Russell, was a traveling fruit tree salesman from Hadley, Massachusetts. On his selling trips throughout the area, he stayed at the Brick Tavern Inn, where he met and fell in love with Evelyn, the innkeeper's daughter. The owner was "Young Gid," the son of the builder, "Old Gid." The couple was married and, on January 14, 1897, Cyrus Russell was born in the brick house to W.H. Russell and Evelyn Julia Reynolds Russell.

In 1922, after a brief stint in the army artillery during the Great War, Cyrus married Hazel Zarr. Their only child, Evelyn, was born about eleven years later. Cyrus had two sisters—Florence, who married into the Cross River Whitman family, and Mary, who married into the local Moore family.

Cyrus Russell served in town government from 1934, when he was elected to the town board, until he retired as town supervisor in 1969. He was called "Mr. Lewisboro" in his time. Upon his retirement, the Cross River Community House was renamed in his honor.

After graduating from Katonah High School in 1913, at age sixteen, Mr. Russell went to work as a carpenter. When the Depression struck hard at the construction industry, he found work as a construction foreman at several Civilian Conservation Corps camps, including the camp located in Ward Pound Ridge Reservation. In 1936, two years after being elected to the town board, he was elected town clerk, a post he held until 1961, when he was elected town supervisor.

Politics wasn't his only interest. He was active in the Cross River Baptist Church, serving as deacon, and he was a founder of the Westchester Christian Endeavor Society, a very active organization at many area churches. Christian Endeavor conducted Sunday school classes and provided social activities for all ages. Mr. Russell was a founder of the South Salem Fire Department in 1938 and was a former commander and chaplain of American Legion Post 129.

During World War II, Lewisboro boasted a very active war council. Mr. Russell was chairman of this body for a time, handing the job over to Supervisor John J.S. Mead in 1942 due to the requirements of his other duties. Cyrus Russell and Chief Warden Pierson Underwood, a writer and movie producer, held training courses for people who wanted to become town wardens. Wardens, according to an official World War II manual, were "the immediate, temporary protectors of life and property in time of sudden disaster or emergency until the arrival of the police, fire, medical and other services, at which time primary responsibility ends, and the warden assists in any way that may be requested." They had to know the location of the public power source and emergency equipment (i.e. sand, axes, ropes, etc.). Thanks to the wardens and their trainers, Lewisboro survived the war extremely well. There were no enemy planes spotted by the plane spotters and all emergencies were taken care of promptly.

Cyrus Russell saw many changes during his political lifetime. Probably one of the most far-reaching changes was the advent of the planning board

Gideon Reynolds's Brick House during its time as an inn, advertising dinner for one dollar. Can't beat that price!

in August 1932. The first zoning ordinance and map were issued in May 1936. These changes created the need for building permits and a building inspector. Three guesses as to who was appointed the town's first building inspector! No contest there. It was the man himself: Cyrus Russell.

The job was part time, but still the hours were long and often crazy. Inspector Russell spent hours riding around the back roads listening for construction sounds. Since most of the construction seemed to be happening on weekends by folks coming up from the city, he changed his work hours so he could more easily issue his stop-work orders and building code violations and handle requests for building plans. Many of the building plans were submitted in pencil, scribbled on odd-sized pieces of paper. These primitive plans can still be found in the early building department files. Cyrus Russell "retired" from that job in 1950, though he remained the busiest official in town for a number of years.

The fifties and sixties were busy years of growth for our town and Cyrus Russell was an important figure in that development. There was continued development around the lakes and the North County Shopping Center was built in Goldens Bridge. Mr. Russell's personal philosophy was: "You can't stop progress but you should be able to control it." He tried to govern by that credo. The town board, under his leadership, appointed an economic development committee to study development problems and the attitudes of local landowners. One of the last things he did in office was to form an advisory committee to develop a master plan for Lewisboro. Unfortunately, his retirement was cut short. He became ill and died on August 25, 1971.

Originally published on March 14, 2002.

The Cross River Baptist Church Endures

A quiet little white church sits on its quiet little hillside on the east side of Route 121 in Cross River. It is an unassuming structure that has provided 201 years of service and worship for members of the Cross River community and beyond. The Cross River Baptist Community Church is the oldest public building in Lewisboro. Other congregations have been in existence longer, but their buildings are younger. None of our public governmental offices can claim a heritage dating back to 1791, the year the Cross River Baptist Church was built by a dedicated group of worshipers.

The church was lucky enough to escape the rising waters of the Cross River Reservoir in the early 1900s; the one-room schoolhouse and the Methodist-Episcopal church had to be moved to make way for the water needs of a growing New York City. The Methodist-Episcopal church, built in the mid-nineteenth century, is now in private hands; it is located just south of the Baptist church, next door to the imposing brick house on Route 121. The Baptist church, with its turn-of-the-century backhouse, stands guard over the entrance to Ward Pound Ridge Reservation. It keeps watch over the comings and goings of Cross River hamlet, secure in its place in the hamlet's history.

On June 23, 1789, just weeks after George Washington took his oath of office as the first president of the United States, a group of members of the Bedford Baptist Church, including Gilbert, Joshua and William Reynolds, joined with Adam Keeling, Elias and Joshua Lee, Ebenezer Ferris, Thaddeus Bronson and Thaddeus Smith (of churches in Stamford and Reading, Connecticut) to organize a new church at Cross River. The group met at the home of Nathaniel Reynolds in Cross River for this purpose.

At that time, the village of Cross River was a thriving community of general stores, a blacksmith, a wheelwright, carpenters, millers and farmers.

It stood at a crossroads of several important highways, including the Danbury Post Road. At first, the congregation met in different members' homes, but before long it decided to raise money to buy property and build a church. Never a wealthy congregation, members raised 130 New York pounds by July 1790, and it was determined that this sum would be sufficient to start the building program. It was decided that the church would stand between Gilbert Reynolds's mill and house, and would be thirty-six feet by thirty feet in size.

An excerpt from the July 18, 1790 church records shows the following labor costs incurred in the project.

> *It was agreed that a Man with a fore Cattel Team and Cart finding himself should have: 0.10 per day; that a man and one pair of horses and cart or wagon finding himself—0.6 per day; that a common Laborer finding himself—0.4 per day; till the first of November then 0.3 per day; that good oake floor Boards should bee—0.6 per 100; that good siding eight inches wide should bee 0.4 per 100; That Steven Wood should be appointed a master workman of said building.*

Work must have progressed well for the little congregation, because the July 3, 1791 church records tell us: "The Church mett [*sic*] at the public place of worship." Through lush times, and lean ones, the church endured. Pastors seemed to come and go with more regularity than those that stayed for more than six months or a year. From 1796 until 1804, Brother Enoch Ferris and Elder Jones supplied the parish as preachers. Brother Fountain of Bedford helped out during that time, conducting services. Asa Bronson preached at the church as well, until 1820, when Brother Bronson joined the North Salem congregation. For the next twelve years, times were hard, services were infrequent, the building was falling into disrepair and "it was a season of darkness to the church."

In 1839, the church leaders decided to completely reorganize. New articles of faith and a new covenant were drawn up. Brother Stephen Holley and Brother George Reynolds were chosen as deacons. The church called the Reverend William H. Card to be its pastor. He accepted in 1840 and began to reclaim the church's place in the village. More than fifty people joined the church and ground was purchased to build a parsonage. Subscriptions totaling $465 were raised for the structure. The church leaders voted "that the house be 32 by 26 feet and that there be a portico." Furthermore, they voted "that the house be painted if Elder Card will get the work of painting done for nothing." In 1846, the congregation still owed $752.82 on the parsonage, which still stands at the southern corner of Route 121

The message on this postcard, circa 1900, explains that the Cross River Baptist Church building escaped the flooding that this part of the town endured for the reservoir.

and Boutonville Road. In 1884, Deacon George Reynolds willed his home to the church for use as a parsonage. The original parsonage was sold in 1888 for $1,200.

A few more pastoral changes took place but, in 1853, Brother David Morris answered the call and another period of growth began. The meetinghouse was repaired and an addition was built on the southern end of the building. This twenty-foot addition included a gallery, a bell tower and steeple. Nathan Banks of Banksville was the carpenter for the work, which cost $1,250. The church, which had started with 8 members in 1789, had 110 members in 1868, even though the Civil War years had been lean. Postwar growth brought prosperity in membership to the congregation.

The Christian Endeavor Society was started in the church in 1915. There had been an earlier society, but membership had petered out. The reorganized group remained the mainstay of the church community well into the 1950s. It was this organization and the Sunday school under the leadership of Cross River Postmaster Chapman Miller (and later Cyrus Russsell) that carried the Cross River Baptist Church through these years. Christian Endeavor provided outlets for community service, religious services and educational and social gatherings for all ages. Mr. Miller's daughter Arvilla was in charge of this organization for many years. There were Christian Endeavor groups in other area churches and joint gatherings were sometimes held, allowing the young folks of the town to mingle and get to know each other.

The interior of the Cross River Baptist Church is as plain and unassuming as the exterior. The staunch white pews with their red-cushioned seats are just comfortable enough to allow the members to attend to the sermon and not doze off. The western light streams in during the afternoons, giving the sanctuary an otherworldly glow. A simple organ sits up front near the pulpit to accompany the congregation as members sing the familiar hymns their grandparents sang many years ago. Although the gallery still stands, looking down on the main floor, its area, which was once used for church suppers and Sunday school, is now used only for storage. The church maintains its dignity and awaits worshipers every Sunday. The congregation is small, but new members are welcomed heartily and services are held weekly, although there has not been a resident pastor for many years.

Several years ago, the little church suffered a furnace blowback, covering the entire interior with sooty, oily ash. It took months to repair the damage and clean every seat cushion, lamp and religious article in the church. The sanctuary had to be repainted from floor to ceiling. During the restoration, old lighting fixtures were discovered, allowing some historical good to come from the disaster.

Descendants of the original members still keep stewardship over the long-lived church. Sisters Lois and Joyce Reynolds, direct descendants of the founding fathers, members of the Moore family and Evelyn Russell (daughter of former Lewisboro supervisor and church deacon, Cyrus Russell) are all leading members of the Cross River Baptist Church. These families are a living testament to the endurance of the faith of the quiet little white church on the Cross River hillside.

Originally published on September 26, 2002.

The Damming of Cross River

We don't usually discuss current happenings in this history column, but the ongoing construction along the Route 35 corridor over the last few months that is causing concern to impatient motorists triggered our imagination and sent it "backflashing" (if there is such a word) about one hundred years, to the time when the Cross River Dam and the resulting reservoir were being built. Now that was a project that disrupted our area for a very long time. These recent months of "Work Zone Ahead" signs and bright klieg lights illuminating the nighttime sky probably can't compare to the disruption caused by the hundreds of workmen, machinery, mules and hubbub the dam construction brought with it beginning in June 1905.

To get a handle on that massive project, we have to journey a little farther back in time, to the mid-nineteenth century. For years, New York City had been wallowing, literally, in one large cesspool. Pollution is not a new phenomenon. The streets of Gotham ran with raw sewage, overflowing cisterns, polluted wells and a grossly inadequate water supply for drinking, industry and firefighting. As a result, diseases like cholera, typhoid and yellow fever were rampant, especially in the summer. Any fire that started in one of the many wooden buildings was unstoppable and entire sections of the city were lost to infernos because there was so little water available to fight them.

Officials in the 1830s knew something had to be done to rectify the situation so they looked north, to Westchester County and to the Catskills. And what did their wandering eyes behold? Why the beautiful Croton River, known to the Native Americans as the Kitchawan River. This nearly one-hundred-mile waterway has its headwaters in the Pawling Mountains in Dutchess County and is fed by numerous streams and smaller rivers. It flows through Goldens Bridge as it makes its way to the Hudson River near Croton on Hudson. The Cross River is a vital tributary to the Croton River.

In 1837, work was begun on the original Croton Dam, six miles above the mouth of the Croton River. The resulting reservoir was to provide the good citizens of New York City with vital gallons of clean, potable water and water to take care of the city's public safety needs. The Croton Dam was finished in 1842, about the same era that the railroad came into this part of the county. Thousands of Irish laborers emigrated from their potato famine–stricken homeland to work on these two monumental projects, hence the start of the area's rich Irish heritage. However, as wonderful as this engineering feat was, the amount of water supplied to New York City was not sufficient by the end of the century, especially after several years of drought in the early 1880s left the city high and dry.

The solution? Another series of dams along the Croton! By 1890, plans were afoot for a dam in Katonah and, ten years later, in Cross River. Between 1837 and 1911, eleven dams were built as part of the Croton water system, including the dams in Katonah, North Salem and Cross River. The tunnels

This postcard, circa 1909, shows the scenic roadway across the Cross River Reservoir dam. The roadway was closed to traffic by the Homeland Security Administration.

for this new series of dams followed a new route toward the city, most of it through Westchester's famous bedrock. Imagine the sights and sounds of the weeks, maybe months, of blasting that such a process required.

A mile-long, narrow-gauge supply railroad was built from Elliott's lumberyard in Katonah to the Cross River dam site. It was known as "the Boutonville Express," and area residents were amused by its not-infrequent trick of tumbling off the tracks and turning over! The tracks ran over a trestle that traversed the "flats" and the Cross River, ending at the height of the dam. Thousands of tons of rock, mortar and lumber were delivered by this "little engine that could."

The New York Water Authority began searching out dam sites and exploring the geology of the area. Residents of Cross River and Bedford hoped against hope that suitable bedrock would not be found; alas, for the farmers, mill owners, shopkeepers and families along the Cross River, a location was chosen and the condemnation of the land was begun. Farms, shops, mills and homes in the surrounding corridor were taken in addition to the land that would actually be flooded. Newcomers of the last eighty years can't imagine what our familiar, busy Route 35 corridor must have looked like when it was mostly farmland—when driving the cows from pasture to pasture along the roadway was a common sight, not speeding SUVs shuttling kids to recreational adventures. Several years ago, when the reservoir was lowered for workers to repair the dam, passersby could just glimpse the outline of stone walls and barn foundations that once stood tall and proud in the fields that are now only a memory.

In February 1905, the announcement was made that a Cross River dam site had been chosen. The July 14, 1905 issue of the *Katonah Times* said that "hundreds of Italians are at work clearing the land where the big dam will be built." This time it was the Italians, not the Irish, who provided the labor for the project. After the land clearing, the framing and stonework commenced that culminated in the beautiful dam we see today. In less fearful times, it was indeed a pleasure to drive or ride a bicycle across the dam road. Nowadays, the area is off-limits for fear of terrorist attack. Perhaps someday we shall be allowed back to enjoy one of our area's prettiest vistas.

Sources say that two hundred Italian laborers lived in shanty towns along the railroad tracks in Katonah and in a makeshift camp near Mount Holly Road. Labor was also "imported" from the South. The June 30, 1905 edition of the *Katonah Times* reported that "next week a force of 400–500 southern colored men are expected." These workers were employed by the McArthur Brothers & Winston Company construction. Two railroad carloads of mules and mule drivers were part of this contingent and occupied what had been, until that time, the George Green stock farm, just east of the dam site. That huge farm is now under the waters of the reservoir.

Dam-building time must have provided enough excitement for the locals. Tempers sometimes flared among the residents of the temporary housing communities. The newspaper was full of reports of fights, and the July 14, 1905 issue of the *Katonah Times* carried the story of a stabbing in one of the shanty towns. In 1906, it was reported that the Mafia had arrived with its attendant shenanigans. More than one murder was reported. To quell the unrest, the sheriff moved his headquarters to a spot near the dam to protect the workers.

Construction of the dam took two years. The dam's gates were closed on August 7, 1907, and the waters began to back up as the reservoir began to fill. By late 1908, the reservoir had filled and a new era began. The "cyclopic masonry dam with its embankments" is 840 feet long, 170 feet tall and 330 feet above sea level. The reservoir holds eleven billion gallons of water. In total it is three miles long and about one mile wide, at its widest point. Cost of the project was $777,741, not much more than the median price of a house in Lewisboro today! The Cross River Reservoir, now almost a century old, is one of Lewisboro's treasures.

Originally published on March 18, 2004.

A Visit to Christmas Past

Recently, a collection of diaries belonging to Chapman Miller, the longtime postmaster of Cross River, was found in a basement in Katonah. The little leather-bound books are in the process of being transcribed and they provide a look at decades of lives lived in that hamlet. The Millers farmed on the hillside just west of the "downtown" area of Cross River, where the highway from Bedford meets the highway from Katonah. The post office and store stood where Yellow Monkey Village is now. The post office is the store to the west of the big barn; the Miller's home is the art gallery.

The oldest diary was written in 1901, when Chapman was fifteen years old. It is the record of a serious young man, a hard worker on the farm and a fervent churchgoer who sometimes attended services three times on Sunday. His dedication to the Cross River Baptist Church continued until his death. Judging from his diaries, life was not easy for the family, but there were sociables, church suppers and entertainments to lighten up the times.

We can get a sense of what was happening in the Cross River of 1901 from Chapman's writing. In 1901, there was no reservoir. There were two streets and a number of houses where the water sits now. Farms were located in every direction. Most families were self-sufficient, except for requiring dry goods and services. Travel occurred by foot or horse-drawn vehicles and the train in Katonah took travelers to New York City.

Chapman seems to have been occupied with farm chores and school. He doesn't talk about hunting or ball playing, pastimes enjoyed by others his age. Christmas was a major happening in the village and preparations in the two churches started several weeks in advance. Chapman first mentions preparations on December 15:

Sunday, Dec. 15—Services as usual today. We are practicing for Christmas now.

Monday, Dec. 16—I went to Carrie's and practiced Christmas music.

Thursday, Dec. 19—Have helped to trim the church tonight (Cross River Baptist Church at the entrance to the Ward Pound Ridge Reservation).

Friday, Dec. 20—Helping at the church decorations.

Saturday, Dec. 21—Still trimming. The church looks ***fine.***

Monday, Dec. 23—The Baptist Sunday School had the Christmas festival tonight. Everything was fine. The decorations were something better than we have had for a good while. I received a little book, a package of candy and an orange.

Tuesday, Dec. 24—The Methodist Sunday School had their entertainment tonight. Their decorations were fine and all was good. I received a book—"With Lee in Virginia," a box of candy and an orange.

For whatever reason, there are no more entries for 1901 so we do not know what young Chapman's actual Christmas was like, but he probably celebrated it with his parents, his older brother, Alex, and his younger brother, Norman. Before the next Christmas, Alex would be gone. He died on June 8, 1902, at the age of twenty-two, from pneumonia contracted as a result of the measles.

The next excerpts are from the 1935 Christmas season. Chapman Miller, now forty-nine, has two grown daughters, Arvilla and Ruth. A third daughter, Laura, died tragically in 1926, at the age of two. Chapman Miller has been Cross River postmaster for many years. The post office includes a bakery and small store. He is assisted by his wife, Laura, who does much of the baking of the bread and rolls that they sell. Christmas and the Baptist church are still the focus of December for Chapman Miller. He sells Christmas cards along with the normal post office services. The postmaster's salary in a fourth-class post office such as Cross River is based on the number of stamps sold, cancellations and other transactions of the office, hence the joy at the large number of cancellations mentioned in this year's entries.

The economy is not good in 1935 and many in the area are just making do. I find it charming and significant that oranges are still an important part of the Christmas celebration.

Monday, Dec. 16—Xmas rush began tonight with five people mailing their parcels. No cards to speak of mailed yet. There have been several other Xmas mailings, but not like tonight so far this year.

Tuesday, Dec. 17—Not much mail this morning but we had quite a good outgoing mail. Cancellations over $11. Getting quite a lot colder tonight. Rehearsing Xmas songs at our house.

Friday, Dec. 20—Bought a small Christmas tree for 50 cents in Katonah.

Saturday, Dec. 21—Mail is holding up to about last year's amount. We have been quite busy.

Sunday, Dec. 22—We used the Sunday School hour in going over the Christmas songs and recitations. It was a cold afternoon although pleasant except for the cold wind.

Monday, Dec. 23—Our Sunday School Christmas program was tonight at the Church. We had a nice program with Jonathan and a Mr. Brown assisting with concert music. The tree and Santa Claus (Lachlan) were especially interesting to the children. We gave oranges to the children besides a suitable gift to each.

Tuesday, Dec. 24—Made rolls and got to bed at 2:30. Got a bridge lamp from Larkin's for Laura.

Wednesday, Dec. 25—Xmas day. Laura baked 8 dozen rolls and I made some ice cream. We had a nice Xmas. Laura, Arvilla & I went to Hawleyville [Chapman's father and stepmother's home]. *Stopped at Josie's* [Laura's sister] *on way home. Got home around 11. Ruth went to a show in the afternoon so she was not with us. I received 2 shirts, tie and shaving articles. Gave Laura a Bridge lamp.*

Thursday, Dec. 26—Put away Xmas cards. Not so many left. William has closed the store [a Cross River rival], *or it has been closed so, for the time being, our business has picked up just a little bit.*

During another Christmas season, in 1936:

Wednesday, Dec. 9—Rehearsal of Christmas songs at our house tonight. I didn't get along very well and attempted to practice alone afterwards. I think maybe it helped a little. My hearing is affected so much that I can't sing as well as I used to, and it troubles me, because I like to sing.

Friday, Dec. 11—Very stormy. Had a rehearsal tonight of Christmas songs.

Monday, Dec. 14—In the evening after closing the P.O., Laura and I went over to Josie's [in Vista]. *Made up bread. Bed about 1 o'clock. Quite a little parcel post going out. Cancellations nearly $10.*

Wednesday, Dec. 16—Mild weather. Nice day, but raining tonight. Practically sold out bread and rolls. Cards mail just beginning to go out. Practicing at Cyrus's tonight. [Cyrus Russell, a neighbor who would become town clerk and eventually town supervisor.]

Saturday, Dec. 19—Not so nice today. Began to storm early in the evening and is a mean kind of night. Adrian Byington gave a Christmas tree for the Sunday School. Cancellations over $9.

Sunday, Dec. 20—We all went to S.S. [Sunday school] *and C.E.* [Christian Endeavor]. *Practiced Christmas pieces at Sunday school and after C.E.*

Monday, Dec. 21—Heavy mail today. Cancellations $28.85. Clara drove the car and Laura and Arvilla went with her to Danbury this evening.

The Cross River Post Office, once the pride of Chapman Miller, is now one of the Yellow Monkey Village shops.

Tuesday, Dec. 22—School Christmas tonight. All went but Clara and I. After I closed the P.O. I went down to the church with the others to get the tree ready for tomorrow night. Didn't make up bread tonight.

Wednesday, Dec. 23—Sunday School Christmas tonight. It was very nice with singing, speaking, and a Christmas tree with Lachlan as Santa Claus. We had ice cream and cake as refreshments.

Thursday, Dec. 24—I had trouble starting the car this morning. Had to be pushed…went to Ryan's [garage in Mount Kisco] *and had some work done on the car to keep the battery charge better. Bought a little Xmas tree for Hawleyville. Laura and Clara went to Danbury and Hawleyville this eve.*

Friday, Dec. 25—Pleasant day and night. We took our dinner with us and all had a nice Christmas together at my father's [in Hawleyville] *between 5 and 6. I got ice from the cove by the bridge and made ice cream and took that, too. Got back after 10 and stopped at Edwin's* [Reynolds, a neighbor] *for awhile. Made up a small batch of bread.*

Chapman Miller celebrated about fifteen more Christmases, a few more than his beloved Laura, who passed away in 1948. After Chapman's death, his daughter, Ruth Rohner, became Cross River postmistress and served in that position for many years.

Originally published on December 17, 2007.

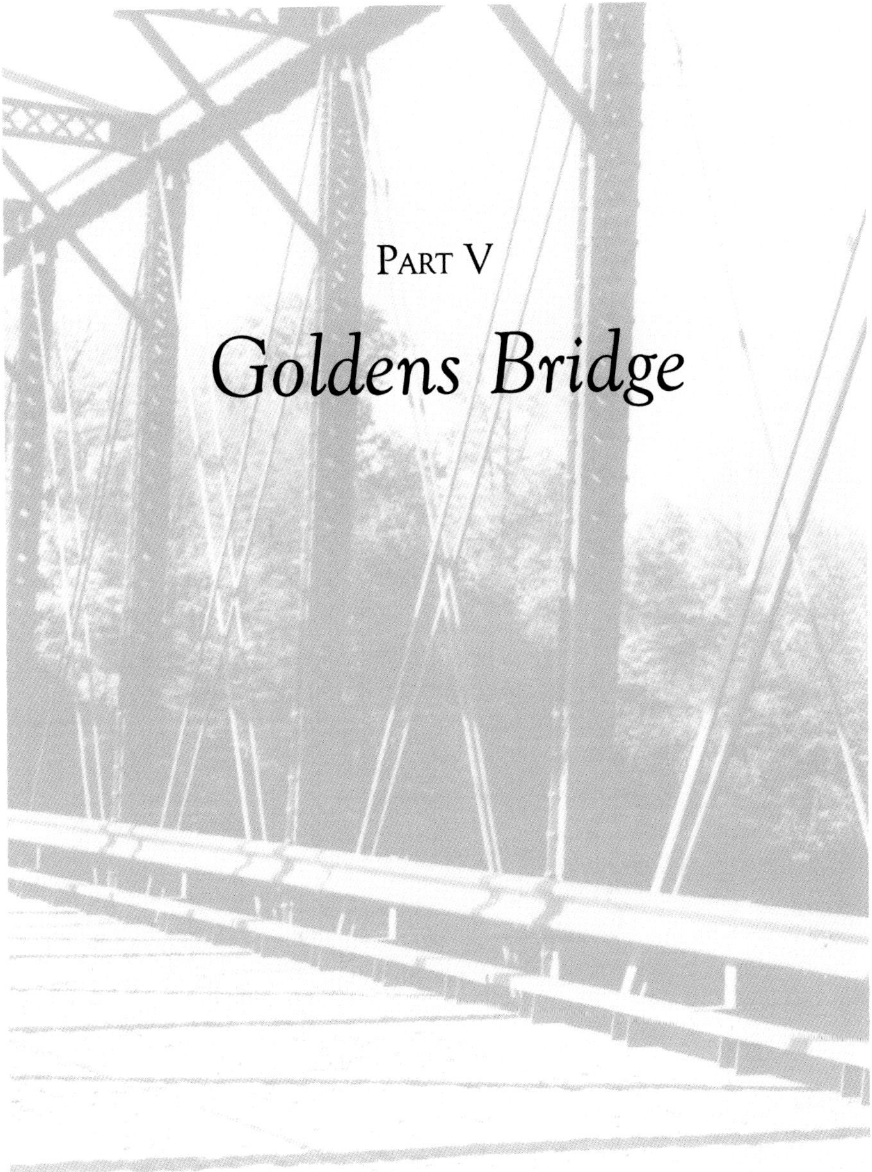

Part V

Goldens Bridge

The Brady Family

The yellow Brady mansion, located on the most dangerous curve in town at the intersection of Waccabuc Road and Increase Miller Road, is a town landmark. This was the home of Simeon Brady, and later his brother, Edward Brady. The Brady lands fanned out east, west and south from that property. The iron gates and fencing are said to have come from New York City—Tammany Hall, in fact. Truth or fiction, we cannot say, but a relative, William Brady, was involved in New York City politics. William served as mayor in 1847–48, although his term preceded the somewhat-tarnished golden years of Tammany by twenty years. However, political friendships endure and who knows the true origin of the legend? The yellow house was built by Simeon Brady (1777–1863). He was an ironworker and carpenter and designed the house with a copper roof. His house replaced the original farmhouse built by his father.

Retreating after the Battle of Ridgefield in April 1777, a band of soldiers stopped at the Brady farmhouse, where they were surely fed and welcomed for the night. Family notes don't indicate how many soldiers bunked down for the night, but Simeon's wife Mary was kept busy throughout the dark hours, baking bread and running bullets (melting down lead) for the troops.

Family tradition has it that two-year-old Mary (nicknamed Polly) woke up during the night and began screaming for her mother, who was definitely occupied elsewhere. The soldiers, spread out across the floor, attempted to entertain and pacify her by passing the child from hand to hand. While preparing this column, I looked more closely at the birthdates of the Brady children, all eleven of them. Little Polly was born in 1782, five years after this memorable event. If I had to select a crying child for this scenario, I would choose Brundage, who was born on August 13, 1774. This same perusal of dates showed that mother Mary was *very* pregnant at the time of the soldiers' unexpected visit since Simeon II was born on May 11, 1777.

But the Brady war stories are not over. The farm, being on a major road, was prey to roving bands of Tories known as "cowboys." These bands of pseudosoldiers, ne'er-do-wells and rogues roamed the countryside, rustling cattle and horses and selling them to the British army to make

The Brady homestead on Waccabuc Road was built by Simeon Brady circa 1800 and was later expanded to the "mansion" pictured in this circa 1900 photo.

some spending money. These fine gentlemen were not above robbing the defenseless families whose menfolk were away fighting in the militia or taking money, silver and valuables, sometimes roughing up the women and children in the process. Often families would hide their possessions at the bottom of a well or under the floorboards and have the older children drive the farm animals into the woods in an effort to save them.

A band of these cowboys invaded the Brady homestead and drove off the cattle, took all the warm clothing that Mary had made from the flax and wool grown and spun on the farm and ransacked Simeon's store, taking much of the merchandise.

Simeon II (born in 1777) married Polly Clayson of Cross River and they had seven children, one of whom was, of course, Simeon III. Simeon II was the one who built the present mansion "as a sort of hope chest" several years prior to his 1827 marriage. He placed his new home about twenty-five feet northeast of the original house, leaving the old house's well in the front lawn, where it still was many years later (and maybe still is today).

Simeon Brady constructed his home from the finest materials available, which meant the house had a copper roof. However, the heat of the summer and the cold of the winter encouraged leaks so Simeon replaced the copper roof with a wooden shingled one. His Scottish heritage wouldn't allow waste so he made three sets of kitchen utensils from the roof copper.

When Simeon II died, the property passed to Simeon III, who eventually sold it to his brother Edward B. Brady about 1880. Simeon III moved to Greenwich with his family. Edward had inherited the farm across the highway from the homestead, and with this large addition he now owned most of the farmland in Goldens Bridge. He was a shrewd cattle dealer and had lucrative cattle and dairy businesses—he often traveled by train to Buffalo to make large cattle deals. There were extensive apple orchards on the farm and Brady applejack cider (hard cider) was well-known, even as far away as New York City, to where it was shipped in large barrels.

The house as originally built was only two stories high. A later remodeling made it into the three-story columned mansion now familiar to passersby. The remains of the millstream and outbuildings are still visible from the highway, especially during the winter.

The Brady family was an esteemed Goldens Bridge dynasty, all of them successful farmers or businessmen. They worked hard and they prospered. The family members were supporters of the Methodist Episcopal Church. Again, family tradition says that it was the Brady family who gave land for the first Methodist Episcopal Church in Goldens Bridge. Hermon Chapel, as the church was known, was located on the present Increase Miller Road. Research has turned up a deed from 1823 showing that Increase and Hannah Miller, another successful Goldens Bridge farm family, sold the land for the chapel and a public school, known as the Hermon Chapel School, to the church trustees for one cent. The trustees at the time included Simeon and John Brady. The Brady family cemetery was located next to the chapel and so was the Increase Miller family burying ground. About 1912 or 1913, Edward Brady, who was one of the founders of Ivandell Cemetery in Somers, had all of the Brady bodies disinterred from the old Brady burial plots in Goldens Bridge and reinterred in Ivandell with new gravestones that obscure some of the history of the family. Some say the deed was a response to a family feud, but since all bodies were removed, perhaps it was because Ivandell was a "modern" cemetery and much more worthy of the Brady family.

Originally published in August 2001.

Remember When?

This week we are going to let "XYZ" return from his resting place in hallowed ground to tell you about what Goldens Bridge was like in the days of his youth, "less than a score of years after the whistle of the first locomotive echoed over its hills and valleys." That would take us back to about 1865 or so since the railroad reached Goldens Bridge about 1848.

The anonymous author wrote an entertaining piece, "Reminiscences of Goldens Bridge," for the souvenir book of the Methodist Episcopal Church, published in 1913. We shall share a portion of XYZ's thoughts with you. Perhaps you might even be inspired to go on a history hunt to seek out the places mentioned by the unknown writer. Here are some clues.

> *The little freight house stood on the West side of the track, with its platform for the convenience of all kinds of produce.*
>
> *On the East side, facing the new road, was a large two-story, flat-roofed building owned by Augustus Clark, which was used for General Store, Post Office, and at one time, a ticket office for the Railroad; later a building was erected on the West side of the track, across from the freight depot, for transacting the Railroad business. After a few years, it was destroyed by fire, and again the railroad business was transacted in the store.*
>
> *Facing the track on the West side was a one-story, basement and peaked roof building owned by Orrin Frost, in which was kept Dry Goods, Groceries, Farm Implements, in fact everything that was needed; here the masculine population gathered on winter evenings, to compare notes, spin yarns, and, apparently, enjoy themselves, for the proprietor was a genial, warm-hearted Christian gentleman; he was succeeded in the business by his son…*
>
> *Just South* [of the depot area] *was a dwelling and Shoe Shop combined, here the young and old hied to have their feet measured and shoes made, for in those days, the making and mending of shoes, was as much of an art, as the Ladies Embroidery of the present day.*
>
> *Just a little further South was a yard where marble was drawn by horses from a quarry East of the village; there it was dressed and loaded on cars and shipped.*
>
> *South on the old highway stood a blacksmith shop, where the clang of the hammer and anvil, rang out in the early morn; later in a larger building*

on the opposite side of the street both blacksmithing and wheelwright business was carried on. Frank Quick, always ready to oblige his patrons, built up a business whose reputation went far and wide. Near he built a home, where with his loving companion he still lives at the age of eighty-four, I think the only residents of former days...

The old highway crossed the R.R. tracks with a wooden bridge, a few feet north of the present crossing, passing eastward behind the present Methodist Church [a veterinary center in 2008].

In the early sixties when the wave of patriotism, and loyalty to country ran high, a flag pole was placed on the east side of track near the store. As the Stars and Stripes were unfurled the school children gathered on the wooden bridge, mingled their voices with the older ones, and sang: "The Star Spangled Banner, long may it wave."

Right here, I am reminded of the collapsing of the iron bridge, just as a two-horse team and sled of milk, was about half way over, the bridge suddenly gave way, driver, team, sled, milk and falling iron were all precipitated to the river below, which fortunately was frozen over...

The little village did not boast of a school-house, the nearest being about a mile North on the road to Purdys Station. Near the Croton Bridge, stood a dwelling where a small private school was held, the rudiments of English

In 1913, Goldens Bridge was a quiet village near the railroad tracks just waiting for progress and prosperity that was slow to arrive.

was taught by one Sister and Music by another, the girls were taught to sew, and the boys the kindly acts which constitute a true gentleman; there being no age limit the wee ones were often tucked away for an afternoon nap.

How loving and motherly they were at the close of the day, teacher and children sang of the "Happy Land Far Away."

One of the enjoyable features of the time was a swing, not one of those easy, reclining affairs, but a strong rope, with board for seat, and fastened to a crossbeam, held by two strong uprights; here young and old inhaled God's fresh air.

For a few years the little village flourished, then the great City of New York needed a larger water supply and the natural windings of our beloved Croton Banks were soon to be overflowed, the grand old trees were cut down, new roads made, bridges built, dwellings, stores and even the church was moved to new sites, and in the place of green fields and old homesteads, we have a beautiful lake. Our village survived the shock, and still boasts of General Stores, Feed, Lumber, and Coal business, a Milk Factory, New Churches, School, and Fire Hall, Blacksmith and Barber Shop, and a Garage. Besides Telephone and Electric Light service and a schedule of train service equal to any along the line.

So ends our abridgement of XYZ's tale of his old Goldens Bridge. Now, take your copy of the Beers Atlas map of 1867 and give a look for the spots mentioned. I must warn you, though, that just about everything has changed except the location of the railroad tracks. Even Route 138 (the old highway) has been straightened and relocated. It no longer goes by either the front or back of the Methodist Church. The Croton Bridge traverses the reservoir as part of Route 138. The road south to Katonah is now a track running through the woods, used mainly by fishermen and those seeking solace from the hum of traffic from I-684. Where there used to be three track crossings, there is now only one. Where there were once woods and wilderness and a few shacks, there is a shopping center. Where there was the lowing of cattle waiting to be shipped out, there is the incessant rumble of seventy-mile-per-hour traffic. Such is progress. Perhaps some of you are writing in your diaries of the Goldens Bridge of the twenty-first century, to leave a record for those who are to come. How will your words and the sights you describe mesh with the memories of 140 years ago? Who will read your thoughts?

Originally published on August 25, 2005.

Schoolmarm in Distress

This being the week of the school budget vote, when the subject of education and our schools are certainly on most everyone's mind, I just happened upon a little gem of a paper in our files on Goldens Bridge. The document is a copy of a court action brought by a young woman (at least I assume she was young) against the sole trustee of School District 5 in Goldens Bridge. The year was 1899; the teacher was Charlotte M. Tobey; and the sole trustee was Silas D. Gregory. The incident almost has the makings of a novel. It certainly has the proper ingredients—a pretty young heroine, a dastardly villain, excited townsfolk and a possible underhanded plot!

Enter our heroine, Miss Charlotte M. Tobey. She is newly arrived in Goldens Bridge, fresh from the Teachers' Agency in New York City. On January 3, 1899, the agency informed Miss Tobey that a Mr. Silas D. Gregory of a distant prosperous farming community was in immediate need of a teacher to start the winter term at his one-room schoolhouse. That school, in District 5, was the Hermon Chapel School on Increase Miller Road, next door to the Hermon Chapel. The school served the farm children in the area, mostly Bradys and Todds. There were probably no more than fifteen pupils at any one time. But a new teacher was needed since the previous schoolmarm from the fall term was no longer on the payroll—I don't know why, but perhaps she had found herself a beau.

Miss Tobey immediately traveled to Goldens Bridge and met with Mr. Gregory. He inquired about her credentials, her schooling and her diploma. She replied that she had an academic course and a first grade license, and had taken a partial course at a state normal school (the forerunner of our state teachers' colleges).

Mr. Gregory asked if she could teach algebra, bookkeeping and music. "Algebra and bookkeeping, yes," she said, "but I'm not sure about music. I've had some training in vocal music, though, and I'm willing to give it a try." She offered to teach for a month so that he might judge her qualifications and, if satisfied, give her a contract for the ensuing seventeen weeks of the term. He asked her to start teaching on Monday, January 9. For her week's labors she would receive ten dollars in wages. In the meantime, she returned to her boardinghouse in Katonah and sorted through her trunk for her license and credentials to show to her new employer. He visited her on January 7, a Saturday, and inspected her credentials and two testimonials. He said he was "perfectly satisfied with what he saw, especially her 100% in

Hermon Chapel School (built circa 1828), on Increase Miller Road, was probably the misguided Miss Tobey's school. The school is no longer standing.

arithmetic!" He said that he wanted her to teach for the remainder of the term, as he didn't want to hire three teachers in one year.

A dark and early Monday morning, January 9, in the cold wintry blast before the sun was all the way into the morning sky, Miss Tobey started on her way to her new position. She declared she would not lodge closer, that she would hazard the five-mile walk each way. Those were the days when the potbellied stove took up the center ring of every classroom. It was a constant job in the winter to keep the thing stoked and the temperature warm enough on the fringes of the classroom to prevent ice from forming in the ink bottles. I don't know exactly what grades she taught that freezing January morn, but she probably had a good mixture of ages and a good many educational challenges. The future seemed secure.

One would assume she enjoyed her position and her chosen profession; but then again, one never knows, looking back one hundred years and reading between the yellowed lines of a court document. Whatever her thoughts, young Charlotte obviously wasn't expecting the school door to burst open at precisely 2:45 p.m. on Friday, January 13, toward the end of the afternoon session, and the large, heavy-coated figure of Silas D. Gregory to appear in the doorway and say, "Your tenure here at District 5 is history!" Mr. Gregory addressed the scholars, "My friends, there will not be any

This cheery room in one of the town's one-room schools is decorated for harvest time. This photo was taken in 1912.

school on Monday. We will let you know when school will again commence. Good day to you all."

After the children had gone, Charlotte said to Mr. Gregory, "I am startled, sir, by your statement to the students. Whatever do you mean? No school on Monday?"

"Yes," he said calmly. "You have not given satisfaction and when school begins again, it will be with another teacher! I shall give you an order for $10 for the week you have taught." A chagrined Charlotte Tobey made plans then and there to appeal her dismissal to the superintendent of public instruction of the state of New York. She claimed she was unfairly dismissed and had been told she would be allowed to teach for a month so that her skills could be properly evaluated. Since no one else was present at any of the interviews between Mr. Gregory and herself, and there was no written document, it was only her word against his that she had been told that she was the new teacher for the next seventeen weeks. Miss Tobey claimed she was owed a month's salary and that she had only proposed the month's trial teaching as a "last resort" so that she would get the position.

On April 5, 1899, Mr. Gregory filed his response to Miss Tobey's claims—he denied all of her claims. He said he told her that since she had paid all her expenses to come to Goldens Bridge, she could stay and try to teach in the school. "If she is satisfactory," he said, "I shall keep her as a teacher!" No specific length of time was mentioned said the crusty gentleman. "She knew I would only allow her to teach as long as I desired her to do so!"

Since there was no written contract, as required by law, there was no proper agreement and Miss Charlotte Tobey was distinctly out of luck (and a job). Mr. Gregory evidently was not pleased with her habits or her work. "It is ridiculous that she would prefer to walk the five miles from Katonah to the school house, especially in the winter when the roads are often impassable on account of the snow and mud. It would be impossible for her to keep school regularly!" he huffed. Mr. Gregory claimed that he had been told by one of the pupils that Miss Charlotte had been put out of the school where she taught last.

The parents were not happy with the hapless teacher, either. Several had called upon Gregory in his study to inform him that their children told them that they had not recited their lessons in two days. The students told their parents that the teacher would not allow them to ask questions—that she refused to answer and told the students to go home and ask their parents. The angry parents told the district trustee that they would send their students elsewhere if he kept the teacher.

Miss Tobey did not bother to answer Mr. Gregory's claims. Instead, she complained that the scholars had "no respect for me. They talked saucy to me and would not mind my instructions. And besides, she added in a snit, "I don't like to teach school, anyway!" So there.

Perhaps it is unnecessary to say that Miss Charlotte M. Tobey's appeal was dismissed by the public school superintendent. She taught for one week; she got her ten dollars; and I don't have a clue as to her successor in the little schoolhouse in District 5.

Originally published on June 5, 2003.

The Colony at Goldens Bridge

In 1565, the Spanish settled St. Augustine; in 1620, we saw the beginnings of the English settlement of the Plymouth Colony; and in 1927, a group of intrepid Russian-Jewish immigrants from the Bronx made their way northward to the pastures of a dairy farm in Goldens Bridge, looking for a summer escape from the brutal heat and hectic pace of the city.

These working-class pioneers dreamed of creating a community based on the principles of cooperation and comradeship. They formed a co-operative and purchased 150 acres of the Lieberman farm in Goldens Bridge for $51,000. The farm, a working dairy farm, was located on Route 22 and Waccabuc Road. For these summertime escapees from the sidewalks of New York, the green pastures and the sights and smells of the country brought golden dreams and memories of lands left far behind.

Membership in the Goldens Bridge Co-operative Farms, Inc. was sought among workers and professionals—no bosses need apply. The minutes of a 1930 organization meeting proclaimed: "Motion to allow bosses and owners of businesses to come into the Colony…if we let in rich members, they will want more improvements which the…workers will not be able to afford…Question referred to the next meeting."

A follow-up from the 1931 meeting: "Motion passed that no employers be allowed in as members, except in special cases."

Each member family pledged a $100 initiation fee, and $10 per month for interest, taxes and the land cost—an acre share cost $700. Later the co-op voted to allow the acre shares to be divided into smaller lots. The group's hope was to "create a humanistic and politically aware environment in which to bring their families during the summer," according to an article in the August 12, 1987 *Lewisboro Ledger*.

The 1920s and 1930s witnessed a number of co-operative community attempts, some more successful than others. The colony at Goldens Bridge has survived them all. What began with a barn, a pond and tents clinging to the hillsides and fields has become a multicultural, year-round community. Times were tough during and following the Depression in the 1930s. Property ownership changed as the economy and family circumstances faltered, but the colony managed to keep its humanistic ideals and its financial head afloat.

The pond was transformed into an eight-acre lake using the manual labor of the men and boys of the community. A day camp program was begun that is still in existence. The change from summer to year-round occupation began in the 1940s, after World War II. The 1950s and 1960s saw steady growth in the community, as second- and third-generation families built homes or inherited the original members' properties.

As the 1930s gave way to the 1940s, the tents gave way to crude barracks-style summer camps and then evolved into more substantial vernacular and Cape Cod–style houses. A drive through the community's roads today reveals a marvelous eclecticism of architectural styles and personal expression.

Continuity is evident along the roads of the colony—Main Road, Lake, Hall, Hillside and Pond Streets. Some families have lived in the colony for four or more generations. The comradery that began the community

This eight-acre lake, built by the original community members, provides year-round recreation for today's colony residents.

endures today. In 1977, on the occasion of the fiftieth anniversary of the co-op's founding, Maxie Arons—the son of one of the founders and a lifelong resident of the colony until his death in 2000—compiled a history of the area, combining his memories, those of many of his neighbors and excerpts from the files and minutes of the organization.

For many of the early settlers, the hour-long train ride from the Bronx to Goldens Bridge was but a short ride on the New York Central to a weekend of bliss. The families would walk, single file, from the railroad depot to their tents, ready for a weekend away from the city's woes. Oftentimes the women and children would remain in the country while the men went off to work during the week. These were people with forward-thinking ideas, strange to the minds of many of their Goldens Bridge neighbors. The colony women would occasionally wear slacks or (perish the thought) shorts to the A&P to do the marketing or go to the drugstore. Ladies just didn't wear shorts to appear in public in those days (the 1930s). The children were often taunted by the boys from the village, called "Jew boys," and often there were brawls. As the years wore on, however, and the kids from the country saw that the kids from the city played baseball, swam and ran the same way they did, mingling took place. Children from outside the colony sometimes attended the day camp, which was the only day camp in the area until the 1960s.

The colony members were individuals who had strong beliefs in social and political causes, causes that were openly leftist in the minds of their more conservative Goldens Bridge neighbors. Many of them were strong union supporters and embraced communist and socialist candidates for national political office. "The people coming to the Colony in the (early days) had political leanings toward the liberal, progressive, left wing...They were Communists, Socialists, Democrats, Trotskyites. A while later we had a Republican or two and even a couple of Conservatives," said Maxie Arons in his 1977 colony narrative. These were the times of sixty-hour workweeks, no child labor laws and sweatshop conditions for workers. Colony members stood on picket lines, carried placards and sang the union songs of Woody Guthrie and Pete Seeger. They voted for Roosevelt.

In 1948, colony members backed South Salem resident Henry A. Wallace for president. Mr. Wallace had accepted the endorsement of the American Communist Party during his campaign. Political activists spoke and folk singers like Pete Seeger appeared in concert at the colony's barn. Freedom of expression was encouraged by all the members.

Bettering themselves educationally and culturally was a high priority. To quote from Maxie Arons's narrative, "Every home had a wind-up phonograph with Caruso records, Yiddish and Russian melodies; and lots of books...They were really strong on books." There was a summertime women's book discussion group that met weekly for many years. It was one of the most important social gatherings of the community.

Saturday evenings were fun-filled for kids, teenagers and adults. The whole community would enjoy folk dancing, food and entertainments, which always began with some sort of political speech and discussion. Often the entertainment was professional, but the members of the community would produce their own plays as well. The highlight of the Saturday events was the refreshment table, filled with ethnic wonders of all kinds. Every homemaker was pleased to share her specialty.

The colony, now known as the Goldens Bridge Association, celebrated a proud seventy-five years in 2002. I will close this column with a final excerpt from Mr. Arons's 1977 narrative: "Many people dream beautiful dreams, but few are willing to work to make their dreams a reality. The Goldens Bridge Colony's pioneers worked, and struggled, and sacrificed. They never lost sight of their goals. They had a dream, and they were determined that, by hard work and cooperative effort, their children, if not they themselves, would see that dream come true."

Originally published on July 25, 2002.

PART VI

Three Lakes Area

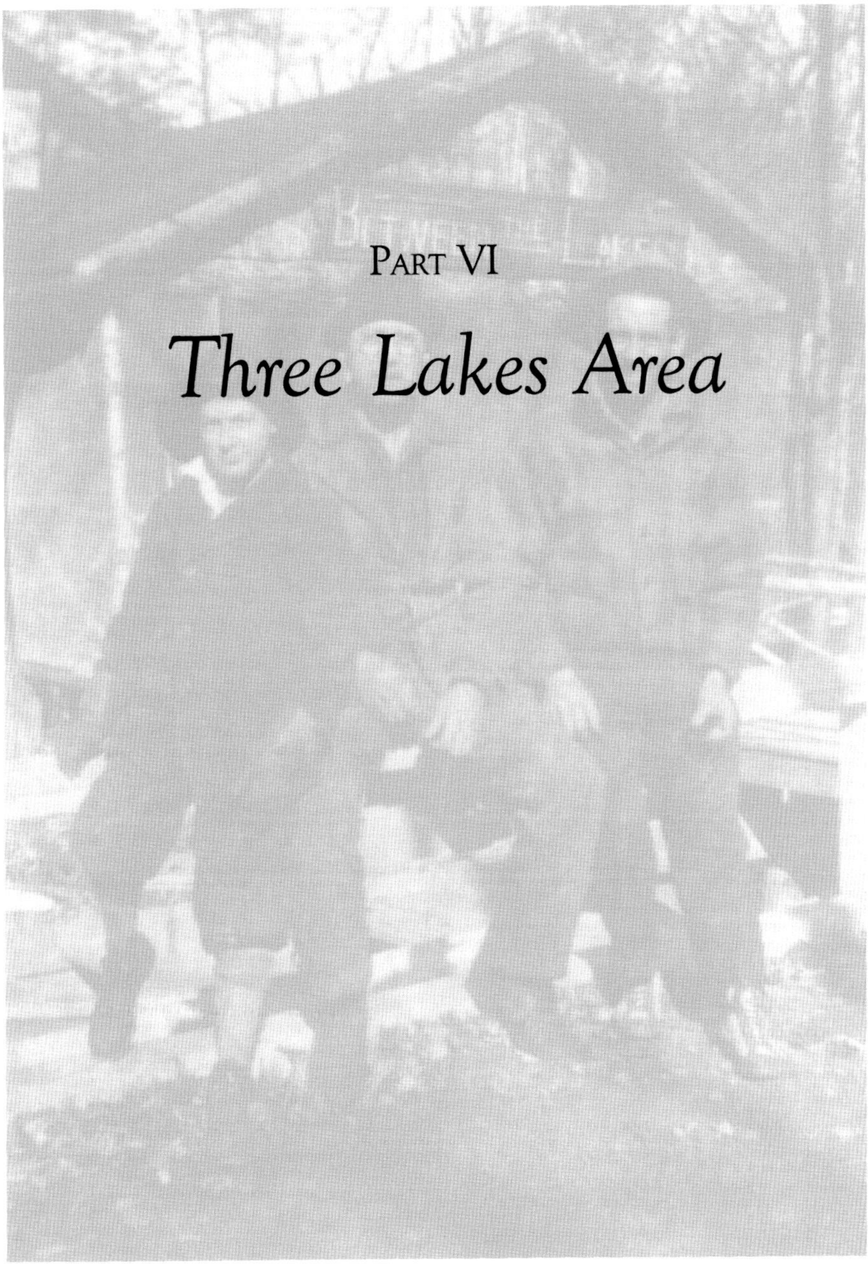

Having a Great Time—Wish You Were Here!

It's summertime and this week's column invites us to a summer sojourn spent in quiet elegance on the shores of Lake Waccabuc in 1867 or 1869 (the date is difficult to decipher). The letter that follows was given to me by Joseph Wittmann, of Somers, a descendant of the writer and of the family who built the Lasdon Estate, now a Westchester County Park. The letter, written on Lake Waccabuc House stationary, is from the time when Waccabuc was a destination listed in the railroad's summer vacation brochure that told of places where residents of New York City could escape the city's doldrums and dangers from disease and the awful industrial pollution and heat. Those with means traveled by train to Katonah or Goldens Bridge and walked or rode by carriage to country inns and hotels in Goldens Bridge, Cross River and Waccabuc.

The Van Norden manuscript, an unpublished history of South Salem, written in the 1920s, said that the hotel property was originally owned by the Benedict family and was given to William Benedict by his father Benjamin sometime after 1836. William lived in the original house until about 1857, when he sold the property to Martin Rockwell Mead. Martin Mead enlarged the house to three stories, adding greatly to it, and opened it as a summer hotel between 1860 and 1865. According to Theodore Van Norden, the name Waccabuc was suggested to Mr. Mead "by the old Indian name of the lake or the name early given to the Indians of the neighborhood." Mr. Van Norden indicates the hotel name then became associated with the lake. After Martin's death in 1882, his wife Octavia continued to operate the establishment until fire destroyed it in 1896. Today, only the former boathouse and bowling alley are still in existence.

Now, imagine a shaded veranda, a portable writing desk and a young gentleman writing a letter to his sister in time for the morning post. The letter is written on house stationery and embossed with the postmark "Lake Waccabuc House, Goldens Bridge, M. R. Mead, Proprietor." The paper is headed, "Lake Waccabuc House, Aug. 15, 1867[or '69]."

He begins:

Dear Annie,

I received your letter of Aug. 12th yesterday. I was very glad to hear that Mother is so much better and now I am anxious to know whose medicine did her good, mine or the quack's! You gave me a very good account of cholera workers in your own case which a good dose of Carter oil would soon have cured. Why didn't the quacks cure Sarah? We have been having gay times here for the last week. One evening Robert Pardow gave an exhibition of magic. The next evening we had tableaux, and wound up the week by having a grand hop last night (Saturday). The ladies and gentlemen decorated the parlor and piazza very prettily. We have a beautiful piazza (going) around the whole house except for one end. This was beautifully decorated with evergreens and colored lanterns. We sent invitations to the guests of neighboring hotels not one of which, by the way, is nearer than six or seven miles, and most of them came. The hop was given by the gentlemen of the house. We imported two musicians and 40 quarts of ice cream from the city for the occasion. The musicians of course had to remain all night, and the proprietor of this house is such a mean man that he obliged us to pay their board. However we had a nice time and it only cost us three dollars apiece.

It is well that you decided not to come here for you would not be able to get a room. The house is full. Mr. Mead had a private house about three quarters of a mile from the Hotel and there are about twenty people lodged there. Last night three gentlemen slept in the stable and two in the bowling alley. (Josie) has a few more friends than he had in the beginning. One old lady has taken a fancy to him. She says that he is a very good boy and is only bad when he is (eased). He has taken wonderfully to ball playing. He saw the boys playing ball one day and the next day, he got his own ball and a big stick and tried to bat the ball as he saw the boys doing. He got quite angry when he could not do it to his satisfaction, but he tried it until he was scarcely able to stand up. We are all very well and send our love to you all.

Yours affect.
Joe

The reader may have been surprised to hear the dance at the Lake Waccabuc Hotel described as a hop, remembering back to teenage times and the sock hops of more youthful days. Actually, the word "hop" was slang or colloquialism for "a dance, a dancing party, especially of an informal or unceremonious kind," as long ago as 1731, when it was used in an English publication.

A reference in the letter to the proprietor as "such a mean man" probably did not defame his character so much as to describe him as a stingy or penny-pinching fellow, one who did not spend money foolishly for musicians from New York City.

There is an interesting reference to what is probably the newly popular game of baseball. The letter writer described how "Josie" had been impressed with the older boys playing with bats and balls, so much so that he has fashioned his own game using a stick and a ball. Recently, the real origin of what used to be known as Abner Doubleday's great invention has come under much debate. Here we have a post–Civil War reference to the game of baseball being played right here in Waccabuc!

Annie, the recipient of the letter, was married to Henry Spingler Van Behren and lived in New York City. She died two years after this letter was written, from cholera, I believe. She was the great-grandmother of Joseph Wittmann.

A handbill advertising the hotel proudly claimed, in bold print, "No Tramps! No Bar! No Malaria!" The *Katonah Record* was quoted as saying, "M. R. Mead, proprietor, spends the winter maturing plans for the comfort and amusement of his summer guests."

The *New York Sunday News* proclaimed, "Already many New Yorkers and Brooklynites have taken refuge from the summer heats here."

The Waccabuc Hotel, at the western end of Lake Waccabuc, provided a fine place to escape the city's summer maladies after the Civil War.

The *Brooklyn Daily Eagle* reported that "within fifty miles of Grand Central Station, our traveler stops at Goldens Bridge station, after a comfortable ride of an hour and a half," for which the regular fare was $1.05; the excursion fare was $1.85. A stage coach awaited the refreshed but weary traveler and spirited him over four bucolic miles past rippling streams and romantic cowsheds to Lake Waccabuc House and its inviting veranda, blessed by gentle lake breezes.

Hotel rates, in 1891, began at ten dollars per week and the cost was dependent on the location of the room and the length of the stay. Transients were charged three dollars per day. Special rates applied to families. Requests for rooms had to be made at least one day in advance and had to include the number of adults, children and servants in the party. The hotel could accommodate up to one hundred guests.

The hotel, operated as it was for almost 30 years, did not seem to leave a permanent impression upon the land. The beach is still used today, the boathouse remains and there are signs of the water system hidden among the overgrown vines in the woods, but the incredible beauty of Lake Waccabuc remains, almost as pristine as it was 140 years ago. One can still paddle a canoe around the six miles of lakeshore, marvel at the Indian ovens and anchor for a picnic lunch in a quiet cove or under the shadow of Castle Rock. The west end of the lake is no longer home to the Lake Waccabuc House, but when summer arrives each year, shouts echo up from the shore and reach out across the lake, proclaiming that there's no better place on earth than Lake Waccabuc.

Originally published on July 19, 2001.

Mead Street

The hamlet of Waccabuc remains unique in its beauty and sense of elegance, combining its remembrance of things past with an acceptance of the present. The aura and heritage of Waccabuc can be summed up in two words—Mead Street.

Although in colonial times, the road was the New York to Vermont post road (note mile marker no. 52 in front of Waccabuc Country Club), there could be no other possible name for a street that was home to the farms of so many members of the Mead family, a family that has played a dominant role in the history of our town. Not only was the family one of means, but it was also one of many offspring, leading to a community populated with aunts, uncles, brothers, sisters and cousins galore! The farmland, woods and mountainsides surrounding Lake Waccabuc have been home to the extended Mead family for more than two hundred years.

The first of the Waccabuc Meads was Enoch. Born in 1725, he arrived in 1776 with his bride. The newlyweds traveled by horseback from Greenwich, were enthralled with the beautiful rolling hills, sparkling lakes and fertile soil and set about building a homestead. The *Mead Memorial Chapel Remembrance*, written in 1957 states, "Enoch and his eight children and his three slaves cleared and farmed the land." When Enoch died in 1807, the real estate was evenly divided between his two sons, Alphred and Solomon; Alphred received the lands south of School House Road and Solomon the part to the north that included the original farmhouse. That homestead eventually became known as Elmdon.

The gracious circa 1780 house sits gable-end to the road on the eastern side, just north of School House Road. The house endured several alterations, including the destruction of the original chimney and much interior detail, according to the Mead Memorial Chapel history. The changes wrought by Robert Hoe, a nephew of Enoch Mead's grandson Harvey, were later corrected by Coralie Brooke, who restored the house to its original condition. The house now sits behind a charming picket fence.

In 1821, Alphred built the present house now referred to as the Mead Homestead. The simple white home adorns the corner of Mead Street and School House Road, behind its own charming fence. Alphred and Polly built this new house because their first home had gotten too cramped for their family of seven children. Alphred Mead maintained the Homestead Farm until his death in 1855. His wife Polly lived there until her death in 1878, and his daughter Loretta remained mistress of the home until her death in 1901.

The Homestead still belongs to a Mead descendant, who has surrounded the former farm with wonderful gardens and a small vineyard. Gone are the horses, cows, chickens and other barnyard animals as Mead Street has settled into a less agricultural, more suburban neighborhood. One finds it easy to imagine, though, one day a century ago, when a stroll or a ride along Mead Street would offer the sights and smells of dairy farming and carriages bringing summer visitors the Waccabuc Inn at the north end of Mead Street.

The Waccabuc Country Club was originally a two-story farmhouse owned by Martin Rockwell Mead, son of George Washington Mead.

One of the enjoyable leisure activities of the summer "campers" was a boat trip through the channels connecting the lakes.

George Washington Mead was the "forefather of the present Meads of Mead Street," according to the 1957 *Remembrance*. G.W. Mead sold the property to Robert Hoe, who altered the house by adding an extra story and a "Victorian addition" about 1865. Mr. Hoe also built a smaller farmhouse, a stable, barns, a log cabin–style playhouse, a carriage house and the Waccabuc Post Office. According to a history of the houses on Mead Street written by David I. Mead entitled *A Bird's-Eye View of Waccabuc Titles*, Robert Hoe "removed all stone walls putting them in the highways and planted privet hedges." Some of the buildings are still in use at the country club.

The land opposite the Mead Chapel at the western end of Lake Waccabuc was once the site of a glorious Victorian country inn known as the Waccabuc Inn. The inn was a blessed getaway for city folk suffering from malaria, the onslaught of mosquitoes and the beastly summer city heat. Railroad brochures enticed travelers with promises of boating, fishing, bathing, rambling, bowling and driving. "Within fifty miles of the Grand Central Depot," said the *Brooklyn Daily Eagle*.

George Rockwell Mead was the proprietor. He bought the property when he sold his farm to Robert Hoe. Shortly after the Civil War, he converted the existing home to a hotel at the head of the lake. After his death in 1882,

Lake Waccabuc Inn is now Waccabuc Country Club. A postal mile marker out front declares the spot to be fifty-two miles from New York City.

George's wife Octavia rented the hotel to various tenants, who continued the tourist business until the entire structure went up in flames in 1896. The inn was never replaced.

In 1891, the cost of a delightful stay at the Lake Waccabuc Hotel was "$10 per week and upward, according to location of rooms and length of stay." Special rates applied to families wishing to spend the entire season at the inn, the season running from May 30 to October. Transients paid three dollars a day. Reservations were made for families, including their servants.

The hotel's brochure regaled Waccabuc Lakes, which included Oscaleta and Rippowam Lakes as well as Lake Waccabuc, and described the area as:

> *The most charmingly romantic spot on earth, especially gifted by nature for a perfect summer resort. Waccabuc Lakes…1,000 feet above the level of the sea, 44 miles from New York City, is one of the most attractive, picturesque mountains of unbroken ruggedness, sweeping valleys, flowing streams, grand old forests, and weird glens, all combined to charm the tourist and busy resident of the city, who desires a season of enjoyable rest, with entire change of surroundings and recreations.*

Planned recreation got its start at the Waccabuc Hotel. Within a couple of decades, the golf course followed and the farms began to disappear. Now

Mead Street counts few Meads among its inhabitants, but the scene is still one of elegance and the gracefulness of times gone by.

Originally published on June 12, 2003.

A Victorian Summer Sojourn

The Orlofsky family of South Salem gave the town an old, decrepit leather case inscribed in gold with the word *Lewisboro*. Inside the decaying leather cover were two wonderful news articles from the *Tarrytown Argus*, one dated September 6, 1890, and the other undated but obviously from the same time. One was titled "Camp Life at Waccabuc" and outlined a week of camp life, 1890s-style; the other, the dated and longer article of the two, "Camping Out," details all there is to do in the camp and in the surrounding towns. The article, signed by "Em Jay," expounded on the glories of Camp Nemo and the three lakes surrounding it. I have a hunch that Em Jay might be M. Josephine Close, one of the camp's inhabitants.

Both articles tell the tale of Camp Nemo, situated somewhere on Lake Waccabuc, most likely on the southern shore. These Victorian-era summer camps were rustic cottages or larger simple dwellings surrounded by trees and nature or the rural countryside.

I will begin with a passage from "Camp Life at Waccabuc":

> *The camp is situated about eight miles from the Village of Katonah. After a long drive over a dusty road, one is greeted by the word, "Welcome" over the porch of the old farm house at the camp. On the front of the house is a large veranda that, with six or seven hammocks hung from its posts, affords good solid comfort to the campers at all times during the day. At night these hammocks are taken down to make room for promenading and dancing. Three pretty lakes are within a short distance from the camp, each of which is connected with the other by small narrow channels. Rowing and fishing on these lakes, driving* [for the younger generation reading this, driving meant real, old-fashioned horsepower, not cars] *over the roads of the country, playing tennis and taking tramps in the woods occupied the time of the "campers." Isaac, the colored cook, attended admirably to the recurring wants of the "inner man."*

Adding to the above is an excerpt from the "Camping Out" piece:

> *We breakfasted at seven, dined at one, supped at seven. Our Caterer was an experienced hand from Danbury, Ct., Isaac Cooper. Every meal seemed to surpass each preceded one; home made bread, biscuit, fresh corn, tomatoes, vegetables direct from the adjoining farm, butter, golden from a dairy of Jerseys, and milk,—we only drank 220 quarts while in camp.*

From "Camp Life at Waccabuc" we learn: "A pleasanter party could not be found than the one that assembled at Camp Nemo, Lake Waccabuc last week. It consisted of some thirty persons, worthy young people, hailing from Tarrytown, Sing Sing, New Haven, New York, Brooklyn and Wallingford, Vt."

The writer of "Camping Out" named the campers as Julia Brooke, Mamie Brooke, Nellie Lawrence, Fanny Powell, Mr. and Mrs. Charles C. Studwell, Clifford Powell, Will V. Kelly, Fred B. Studwell and Robert Brooke, all from Brooklyn.

He continued:

> *Carrie Hunt of Lake Waccabuc, "Nan" F. Van Duesen of Wallingford, Vt., Mabel M. Studwell, M. Josephine Close, Eloise Linson of Tarrytown, Robt. Fancher, Charles Robinson of Sing Sing, George Lawrence of South Salem, Dr. Archibald McNeil of New Haven, Ct., James N. Andrews, Lewis A. Storrs, J. Hathorne Thompson, John Quinn and Paul C. Morton of New York, and our pleasant good "Aunt Mary" Pierson of Brooklyn.*

Aunt Mary Pierson was the chaperone of the camping party. She was the perfect chaperone, with "the keen eye of a watchful mother, at the same time she was, while fulfilling her mission, really one of us in all our enjoyments."

Many of the campers' names can be found in the annals of South Salem and Waccabuc. Perhaps, for some, it was the wonderful times had at one of these summer camp sojourns that encouraged the family to settle here after the bloom of youth had worn off. Many had personal ties to the area and others were friends from the city, dying to come to the country for some "rest and relaxation."

Friends and neighbors came to call on the campers, especially on the weekend, at the end of a long week's work in the hot, teeming city. The "Camping Out" article describes an unexpected visit and the easy hospitality the visit inspired.

Staying at a summer camp on one of the three lakes meant a festive time for the younger crowd. Anyone for tree climbing?

These nineteenth-century summer campers are relaxing after a bit of frivolity. Note the elaborate costumes and Isaac the cook standing nearby.

Others from the surrounding neighborhood for miles around called for an hour or so, but on Friday night about lamplight in drove three vehicles, with a "heigh-ho!" the camp at once was all life, and "who's there?" Well, we soon found out, for a livelier old party I guess never drove up to that house before. Dr. and Mrs. J.J. Linson, Mr. and Mrs. John Henry Hull, and Mr. and Mrs. E.A. Studwell were there.

Since there was "no room at the inn," so to speak, lodging was found for the visitors at the neighboring Pardee home on account of most everyone being related to the Hulls (Mrs. Pardee was a Hull) in one way or another—and a Hull certainly can't turn away another Hull, so let the partying continue!

The campers spent their days roaming the environs, visiting the villages of North and South Salem and Ridgefield. The ridges and valleys were of particular interest to these "down county" folks and their jaunts are well described:

From our camp we rode westerly along the southerly side of Lake Waccabuc upon a ridge of land, farm lands of Mr. Elbert A. Mead that commanded an extensive view north, west and south, a distance of 20 miles. What a site for a villa. The Waccabuc House was in full view to the north. This house was formerly the farm house of Mr. William Benedict of Unionville. Mr. Benedict sold the property to Mr. M. Rockwell Mead, who rebuilt and enlarged it for hotel purposes and when Mr. Mead was living no stranger was ever turned away hungry and footsore.

A travel guide published by the New York Central and Harlem River Railroad contained a travelogue by one of the inhabitants of Camp Nemo. The pamphlet describes a marvelous ride through the charming village of South Salem, "a small village without any special mark of interest to a stranger; it antedates the revolution a century. The residents are and ever have been noted for their longevity and strictly moral and religious habits, a license for liquor having never been granted in the township."

The Camp Nemo pleasure-seekers of September 1890 planned to follow the jaunts so invitingly outlined in the railroad pamphlet. Here is a summary of their exploits:

Quite a large portion of our party desiring to see the points of interest mentioned in the guide book as quoted started out with every requisite for a long ride, over the ragged hills, through the cultivated valleys and along the high plateaus of rich farming lands that everywhere abound in this

St. John's Episcopal Church on Spring Street in South Salem was described by Victorian campers as "the stone chapel erected in the fifties."

vicinity. From the camp, we rode in a southerly direction, winding along, crossing and re-crossing the serpentine outlet stream of the three lakes as it goes murmuring on to join the many streams that hereabout abound in the famous Croton watershed. The scenery along the highways and by-ways of this entire section is remarkably picturesque and beautiful… We first halted near the stream to visit an old Indian burying ground that lies adjacent to the road; only one white man is buried here, and he was killed at Bedford during the Revolutionary struggle.

We then took the old Boston Post Road to South Salem. West of the village stands a stone chapel, erected in the fifties by the Episcopalian Church in hopes of building up a parish, but there was too much of Presbyterianism here for its growth, and now the building is going to pieces.

After stopping in the old White Church churchyard, the group continued toward Ridgefield. "It would be impossible to describe Ridgefield, but must say that it is a pretty village, handsome villas, large grounds and streets well shaded by mammoth Elms."

The party doubled back after their exploration of Ridgefield and ended the day exhausted. "After hours of riding we reached our camp, ready for Isaac's good supper."

Originally published on May 26, 2005.

Mountain Lakes Park: Rustic Mountainside Retreat

How one views Mountain Lakes Park depends on when the individual first came to Lewisboro. There is evidence of habitation in this remote area shared jointly by North Salem and Lewisboro dating to prehistoric times.

The area was purchased in 1708 from Chief Catoonah of the Tankiteke sachemdom of the Wappinger Confederacy by settlers from Norwalk. Originally, the territory was part of Connecticut until the Oblong dispute was settled circa 1731. The majority of the land that centuries later became Mountain Lakes Camp was purchased in 1727 from the Long Pond Indians, the inhabitants of what is now the Lake Waccabuc area. Among the major purchasers were the Reverend Thomas Hawley and Jonah Keeler. The Keelers settled the northern section; the Hawleys settled the eastern portion. The many stone walls in the park show evidence of farming by these early settlers even though the land is incredibly boulder-strewn in sections. Immense areas seem to be glacial dumping grounds, especially on the mountain slopes running southward toward the shores of Lake Rippowam.

With four lakes and innumerable rippling streams tumbling down the rocky mountainsides, the landscape provided resources appreciated by itinerant Indians. Fertile hunting and fishing grounds and an abundance of berries and nuts to gather made the area as inviting to our ancestors of three thousand years ago as it is to us today.

About sixty years after the first settlers displaced the original inhabitants, a rather unique personality began to call the mountainside home. For thirty years, Sarah Bishop lived alone in a cave overlooking Lake Rippowam, with only the wild animals as companions and an occasional hunter to break the silence of her existence. Tales passed down through the generations say that Sarah appeared in the area about 1780. She was described as a pretty young woman with clothes befitting a gentlewoman of means. She was thought to be from Long Island and had come to the town to escape the terrible trials of the Revolutionary War in her hometown. It is said that Sarah Bishop chose her mountain retreat so that she could look out over the valley below and see the fifteen or so miles southeastward to her beloved Long Island on the horizon.

A romance that was all too short played into the life of Henry B. Anderson, provider of the public water supply for Ridgefield. He purchased the property at the turn of the twentieth century and built a twenty-room mansion, but after the sudden death of his wife, he abandoned the rustic home overlooking Lake Rippowam. He left the home and its furnishings to the adventuresome escapades of local teenagers. The last remnants of the mansion faded away in the late fifties. The house was near what is now called Sunset Point, a lovely spot for watching the sun fall below the western horizon, another reason for romance to be kept alive at Mountain Lakes Park.

The writer has it on good authority that the area was something of a local lover's lane for high school kids in the '60s and more than one tree mysteriously fell across the road, blocking the exit of the young lovers racing to get home before curfew.

H.B. Anderson tried unsuccessfully to develop the area as a high-class resort community in the 1920s. After the failure of that plan, the land was left alone until the 1950s. Interest was revived after World War II and development of about nine hundred acres for family homes was proposed by Mountain Lakes of Westchester, Inc.

About 1959, the Westchester County Board of Supervisors, forerunner to the Westchester County Board of Legislators, proposed acquiring the land as a summer camp for the children of Westchester County. In 1961, 1,083 total acres were purchased or acquired by condemnation proceedings by the county; rumors flew and development of the property began.

Lake Waccabuc is still a beautiful sight from Lookout Point, but the trees have grown up and houses now dot the landscape.

The camp opened for its summer visitors in the summer of 1965. Until 1994, Mountain Lakes Camp hosted sleep-away campers from down-county cities and towns. Disadvantaged and handicapped youngsters were given a place to spend two weeks in the wilderness of our beautiful mountainside locale, swimming and boating in the lakes. For a while, the county ran a music camp at the Mountain Lakes site.

Although most Lewisboro residents don't even know of the camp's presence, and those that do view its presence as nonthreatening, the 1950s summer camp proposal was not welcomed by the residents of the recently developed Twin Lakes community. Angry letters flew back and forth between South Salem residents and the county executive's office in White Plains; rumors sprang up along Lake Rippowam, the area most impacted by any development plans.

An article in the November 22, 1959 *New York Sunday News* claimed that the "Battle of Lake Rippowam" was fast developing. One rumor even told of a railway that would deliver campers down the rock escarpment to swim and boat in Lake Rippowam. Other whispers of misinformation had the camp being used as a camp for "juvenile delinquents" as per Governor Rockefeller's orders. A petition was submitted by the Twin Lakes Association to the supervisors, "protesting these condemnation proceedings to establish a campsite for children." The petition mentioned the possible delinquency camp and the presence of a nearby boat livery and eating facility, which would present an attraction for the campers, as the only "public eating place and boat livery within walking distance of the proposed 87 acres in the Town of Lewisboro."

The residents were worried that the proposed development would affect their existing artesian wells and crowd the lake with campers' boats. The petitioners felt their privacy would be compromised, too.

In a recent conversation with Dr. Eugene Tedaldi and his wife, Annemarie, the couple said that at first, some of these concerns were realized. "Kids came and sat on our dock," said Mrs. Tedaldi. "I was afraid that it was too dangerous for them to swim all the way across the lake. How good were they as swimmers?"

"We [the neighborhood] were somewhat concerned our houses would be broken into by curious campers coming across the lake without supervision," said Dr. Tedaldi. Dr. Tedaldi, who first came to Lake Waccabuc as a child, remembers happy times hunting deer, grouse and partridge in the Mountain Lake hills. "The trout fishing was pretty good, too," he said. "But you had to watch out for Eddie Kirker, the game warden. He would come after us in a boat to check our licenses."

All's well that ends well. Let's hope these ladies have hooked something good for supper from the bridge over the new Goldens Bridge reservoir.

In retrospect, the coming of the camp was the saving grace for the rocky northern hillside border of Lewisboro. The land has remained relatively undeveloped. It escaped what could have been several hundred houses if the developers had had their way. Lake Rippowam, the smaller of the twin lakes, has retained its privacy, and property values have only escalated. Lakefront property that was purchased in 1956 for $5,500 with a house built for $25,000 upon it is worth many times that investment now.

The county is developing a master plan for its Mountain Lakes Park. The area is part of a county biodiversity study that will preserve its unique habitat. The park offers many hiking, fishing, biking and cross-country skiing opportunities that should not be missed by Lewisboro residents. The highest mountain in Westchester keeps watch on the area—Bailey Mountain reaches 982 feet skyward, just over the North Salem border. Mountain Lakes Park is an area rich in human and natural history and should be protected for years to come.

Originally published on September 19, 2002.

Sources

There are too many individuals, articles and books that have been consulted over the eight years of writing my "Window Into History" column to list or even remember. Therefore, this list contains the most important and readily available printed resources used.

Bolton, Robert. *History of the County of Westchester.* New York: Charles Roper, 1881.

Jordan, Alvin, and Koehl, Maureen, eds. *A History of the Town of Lewisboro.* Saline, MI: McNaughton & Gunn, Inc., 1994.

Miller, Chapman. Diaries from 1901, 1935–36. Privately owned. Transcripts available in the office of the Lewisboro town historian.

Scharf, J. Thomas. *History of Westchester County, N.Y., Including Morrisania, Kings Bridge, and West Farms.* Philadelphia: L.E. Preston & Co., 1886.

United Nations Survey. *Town of Lewisboro*. 1946. Available at the Lewisboro town clerk's office.

Van Norden, Theodore Langdon. *South Salem Gravestone Inscriptions*. South Salem: published by the author, 1926.

———. *South Salem History and Traditions*. Unpublished manuscript, 1927.

———. *South Salem Soldiers and Sailors.* South Salem: published by the author, 1927.

The following persons were also interviewed over the course of eight years:

Carl Madsen
Alton Moore
Evelyn Russell
Louisa Tine
Frieda Halpern
Alicia Kellogg
Eugene and Annemarie Tedaldi
The Hans Bauer family
Olin Collier Bell
Mary Ellen Jackowski
Elisha and Lois Keeler
Oliver Knapp
Carol Lawrence
Lois and Joyce Reynolds